Richard Shagner

48

W9-DII-376

SPECIAL PLAYS FOR SPECIAL DAYS

30 MINUTE HOLIDAY & SEASONAL PLAYS

by Judy Truesdell Mecca

Incentive Publications, Inc.
Nashville, Tennessee

Cover and illustrations by Susan Eaddy
Edited by Sherri Y. Lewis

ISBN 0-86530-203-0

TABLE OF CONTENTS

AN OVERVIEW

SPECIAL PLAYS FOR SPECIAL DAYS contains a collection of seven plays for elementary children. There is one play each for the first day of school, Halloween, Thanksgiving, Christmas, St. Valentine's Day, St. Patrick's Day, and Easter.

Some of the plays are just for fun. All have a message and/or incorporate learning activities to increase language skills. Included is a chorus or similar group project to allow for flexibility. Each play is under 30 minutes long.

Necessary information for each play such as scenery, costumes, and props is included, and the minimal cost for the materials should fit into almost any school's budget. So, not only does each play list what you will need, it usually requires items already in the classroom or those that can easily be brought from home. Some scenery can even be drawn on the chalkboard!

Educational materials that correlate with the lesson in each play are included, and vocabulary words that may be new to students are listed, also.

Most of all—have a good time! All actors should learn their lines and work seriously, yet strive to keep the fun in putting on a play.

THE BAGHEAD

THE CAST

- **Narrator**

- **Barry Brizenbean** *(a new boy in school)*

- **Brandy**

- **Chris**

- **Mrs. Kennedy** *(the teacher)*

- **Megan**

- **Tamara**

- **Sean**

- **Mike**

- **Joe**

- **Nick**

- **Additional class members**

- **"Baghead Chorus" members**

NOTES TO THE TEACHER/DIRECTOR:

The Baghead is a short play which deals with the problem of new students being accepted by fellow classmates. It is the story of Barry Brizenbean, the new kid in school, and the difficulties he encounters. He proves his point by painting a funny face on a paper bag and wearing it to school. One student named Nick befriends him. Nick, too, wears a bag, and together they make the point that the rest of the class has not tried to see the "real Barry."

Include as many students in the classroom scenes as you would like. Speaking parts are included in the cast list. The final scene is a song which can be sung by all participants. Have your students create their own paper bag masks and wear them for the final song.

There are several places throughout the play to insert the name of your hometown, the teacher's name, etc.

Words used in the play which might be new to students include:

audience	exclude	narrator	props
continue	exits	old-fashioned	snubbing
dangerous	include	pantomime	

The class should become familiar with these definitions before performing the play.

PROPS

- Suitcase
- Miscellaneous books and pencils; supplies students would carry on their first day of school
- An old-fashioned lunch kit
- Lunch trays with imaginary food
- P.E. equipment (balls, jump rope, etc.)
- A "baghead" for each student in the play (a paper bag with eyeholes cut)

SCENERY

The play takes place in a schoolroom, on the playground, and in the lunchroom.

COSTUMES

Students should wear normal school clothes. In the final "baghead" scene, NICK and BARRY should wear clothing as close to identical as possible, such as white T-shirts and jeans, etc.

MRS. KENNEDY should be aged by putting some baby powder in her hair. She should wear a dress or a skirt and blouse.

TEACHING MATERIALS:

I. Have your students bring brown paper bags from home, and using construction paper, scissors, glue, crayons, crepe paper, buttons, etc., have them create their own baghead masks to wear in the final scene. Be sure to cut functional eye and mouth holes.

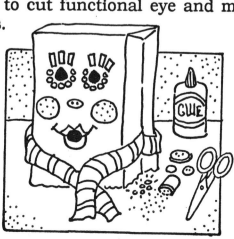

II. The plot of *The Baghead* is followed by the narrator. Explain to your class that a narrator is a character in the play not directly involved in the action of the story but one who helps move the plot along by telling what comes next.

Then rent a videotape or film of a performance of Thornton Wilder's *Our Town*, a play which utilizes a narrator character (called the stage manager). Show it to your class to illustrate how the narrator is used.

III. After explaining that pantomime uses motions and gestures to represent an action (such as pantomiming eating a meal rather than actually eating it), allow them to pantomime the following activities in front of the class:

• putting on shoes and socks

- sewing on a button

- driving a car

- putting in a contact lens

- trying on clothing

- combing someone's hair

- playing a record

- vacuuming

- playing video games

- raking leaves

- planting seeds

- setting the table

- carving a pumpkin

- arranging flowers

This activity can become a game! Write the activities on slips of paper, and have each student draw one from a hat. Divide into teams and have teammates try and guess what each activity is. The team with the most correct guesses wins. (Remember to stress that they are pantomiming these actions.)

Words by Judy Truesdell Mecca

"The Baghead Song"

Music by Jenifer Truesdell Christman
and Woody Christman

with a swing (♫ = ♩ ♪)
♩ = 120

1. Don't judge some-one by the way that he looks. You know what they say 'bout the covers of books. Take time to know him, he might be real-ly nice. And you wouldn't know if you had-n't looked twice.

2. If a new girl comes to live in your town, you should get to know her just sit her right down. Then you just ask her what she likes to play. She might turn out to be your best friend some - day!

3. There's some-thing good 'bout 'most ev - er - y one. Trying to find it can real-ly be fun. Thank you for com-ing to see our play. Now don't treat an-y one like a bag-head to-day!

THE BAGHEAD

A Play about the First Day of School

NARRATOR: Good afternoon (morning), ladies and gentlemen, and welcome to our play *The Baghead.* It is the story of Barry Brizenbean (**BARRY** appears), a nice, somewhat good-looking...

BARRY: Somewhat?

NARRATOR: Well, OK, a **very** good-looking boy who moved from one state (**BARRY** stands on one side of the stage and picks up a suitcase) to _____ (insert the name of your state here). (**BARRY** moves across the stage, faces the audience, and puts down his suitcase.) He was sad to leave his friends back home (**BARRY** waves offstage), but he looked forward to seeing _____ (insert something for which your state is famous, e.g., oil wells in Texas) in his new home.

(As the **NARRATOR** says the next portion of his speech, at least ten students enter the stage and line up two or more rows of desks, like a classroom, and sit in them.)

NARRATOR: When school started, Barry was assigned to Mrs. Kennedy's third grade class (your name and grade may be substituted). Barry took a seat near the back of the room and looked around at his new classmates.

BRANDY: Who's the new kid?

CHRIS: I don't know, let's ask him. Hey kid, who are you?

BARRY: My name is Barry Brizenbean. What's yours?

CHRIS: What's it to ya?

(**CHRIS** and **BRANDY** laugh and pay no more attention to **BARRY.**)

MRS. KENNEDY: (Entering.) Good morning, class! May I have your attention, please? I hope all of you enjoyed your summer vacation and that you have returned to school rested and ready to work.

MEGAN: (Under her breath to **TAMARA.**) I hate it when teachers say that.

BARRY: Me, too!

MEGAN: I hate it when people try to get into conversations where they're not wanted!

BARRY: Sorry...

(The girls giggle.)

12

MRS. KENNEDY: Girls, would you care to tell the whole class what you find so funny?

MEGAN: No ma'am.

MRS. KENNEDY: Then I'll continue. I hope we'll have a great school year.

TAMARA: But speaking of funny, look at the new kid's lunch kit!

BARRY: What's wrong with my lunch kit?

MEGAN: It's just a little bit old-fashioned, don't you think?

BARRY: I didn't think so...

MRS. KENNEDY: Young man, what is your name?

BARRY: Barry Brizenbean.

MRS. KENNEDY: You're new to our school, aren't you, Barry?

BARRY: Yes, ma'am.

MRS. KENNEDY: Well, don't get off on the wrong foot by talking in class on the first day of school! Do I make myself clear?

BARRY: Yes, ma'am.

MRS. KENNEDY: Good. Now, I need to correct a mistake on your supply list. It says "vanilla paper," but it should say, "manila paper." There is no such thing as "vanilla paper."

(**BARRY** laughs out loud and the whole class whirls around to look at him. He turns to the audience and says:)

BARRY: I want to go home!

(As the **NARRATOR** reenters and begins speaking, the boys and girls clear away the desks and get their gym equipment. They begin jumping rope, bouncing balls back and forth, etc.)

NARRATOR: I'm sorry to say that it continued like this for the rest of the day. Each time Barry tried to take part and join in with the other students, the boys and girls excluded him and made him feel like a real outsider. At recess, the boys and girls began choosing sides for Red Rover...(**NARRATOR** exits.)

BRANDY: Let's play Red Rover! I'll be team captain!

SEAN: I'll be team captain! Start choosing teammates.

BRANDY: OK. I choose...Chris!

(The two captains, one by one, pick all the boys and girls except **BARRY**. Then they begin to play and **BARRY** is left at the side of the play area.)

BARRY: How about me? I'm pretty good!

SEAN: Brandy, did you hear something?

BRANDY: No, it must be the wind!

NICK: (Leaving the Red Rover game and crossing over to **BARRY**.) Hey, Barry! That's your name, isn't it?

(While **NICK** and **BARRY** talk, the boys and girls quietly play Red Rover. They continue playing until **NICK** rejoins them.)

BARRY: Yeah, that's right.

NICK: I want to say I'm sorry for the way our class is acting. I don't know what their problem is!

BARRY: I wish they'd give me a chance.

NICK: Well, I've lived here all my life, and now I'm not too proud of that! You seem like an OK guy!

BARRY: I am, if I do say so myself.

NICK: Well, don't worry about it. They'll come around. I guess I'd better get back to Red Rover. I'll see you in class!

BARRY: OK, bye!

(The **NARRATOR** reenters the stage. As he speaks, the boys and girls clear away the gym equipment and push several desks together facing the audience to form a lunchroom table. They sit down and pantomime eating.)

NARRATOR: Now, why on earth would they not want to include Barry in their game of Red Rover? (**BARRY** crosses to the **NARRATOR**.) He's physically fit as you can see. (**BARRY** makes a "strong man" muscle.) He probably plays fair. Don't you?

BARRY: Always!

NARRATOR: Do you think it was just because you were the new boy and they didn't know you?

BARRY: Yes, I think so. But that was not fair! I didn't know any of them either, but I wanted to get to know them! How do you know who's nice and who's not if you don't give everyone a chance?

NARRATOR: Good thinking, Barry. Too bad the other boys and girls weren't as good thinkers.

BARRY: Well, it got worse at lunch.

(**BARRY** takes his tray and joins the other boys and girls at the table. The girl he sits closest to looks at him and scoots away, giggling with the others.)

BARRY: (To audience.) Here goes...(to **MIKE**). So, do you like going to school here?

MIKE: I don't like going to school anywhere, and if you do, you're just a goon.

BARRY: I guess I'd rather be doing something other than going to school, like skateboarding! Do you like to skateboard?

MIKE: Are you kidding? Too dangerous. I'd fall and break my neck.

BARRY: Oh. But as far as school goes, don't you think this one's OK? Mrs. Kennedy seems pretty nice.

MIKE: I guess she is...

JOE: Hey, Mike, who's your friend?

MIKE: He's not my friend. He's the new kid. He's just talking to me.

BARRY: I have a name! It's Barry.

JOE: Like a dog **buries** a bone? Ha! Ha! Ha! (He and **MIKE** laugh.)

(**NICK** is sitting farther down the table and overhears the conversation. He goes to give **BARRY** a hand.)

BARRY: Hey, Barry! How's it goin'?

BARRY: I've had better days. Like the time my dog bit me.

(**NICK** and **BARRY** laugh.)

NICK: So, where do you live anyway?

BARRY: Over on Meadow Lane.

NICK: I know where that is. There's a baseball diamond across the street.

BARRY: That's right!

NICK: Well, what do you say I come over on Saturday morning and we'll hit a baseball around?

BARRY: Sounds great!

NICK: OK! Well, I've got to run. I promised Mrs. Kennedy I'd clean her chalkboards for her when I got through eating. I'm such a nice guy! See ya!

BARRY: Bye, Nick. (To **MIKE** and **JOE**.) Hey, Mike! Hey, Joe! Do you guys want to come over Saturday and…

MIKE: (Cutting him off.) I'm busy…

JOE: Yeah. I've got to…um…

MIKE: He's got to sleep late!

JOE: I've got to clean my room!

MIKE: I guess we'd rather clean our rooms than hang out with you, Barry!

BARRY: (To audience.) I give up!

(All the boys and girls except **BARRY** exit. They clear the lunch trays but leave the chairs as they are. **BARRY** crosses to the **NARRATOR** who has reentered.)

NARRATOR: Don't give up! Not yet!

BARRY: I keep trying to talk to them, but they don't want to have anything to do with me. Only Nick will give me a chance. Maybe the rest of them are right! Maybe I am a creep!

NARRATOR: Now, Barry, how many days have you gone to this school?

BARRY: Um…one.

NARRATOR: One day doesn't seem like a very long time to me. You're not a creep, they just aren't trying to get to know you.

BARRY: They're ignoring me!

NARRATOR: They're not even trying to see the nice, smart...

BARRY: ...good-looking, athletic...

NARRATOR: Come on, Barry. Let's not overdo it! They're not trying to see the real you.

BARRY: I've got an idea! But, I'll need Nick's help. (He exits.)

NARRATOR: Barry had an idea that would make the other boys and girls see his side. Let's watch!

(The boys and girls reenter and rearrange the desks in rows again, like the first scene. **BARRY** and **NICK** are not there. After the other boys and girls take their seats, **NICK** and **BARRY** enter wearing very similar clothing – jeans, white T-shirts, etc., and paper bags over their heads! They take their seats. All the boys and girls turn to look at them, and some giggle.)

MRS. KENNEDY: (Entering.) Good morning, boys and girls, and welcome to the second day of school. I hope you all had a good night's sleep and have returned rested and ready to get to work. (Noticing **NICK** and **BARRY**.) Boys! What are those bags doing on your heads?

BARRY: (Standing.) Mrs. Kennedy, please forgive me and my friend for calling attention to ourselves in class. I know that's not good to do. But we're trying to make a point.

NICK: (Also standing.) One of us is Nick whom you've known all your lives, and one of us is Barry whom you've just met.

BARRY: We're both great guys, not perfect...

NICK: Speak for yourself...

BARRY: We're both pretty good guys, though, and as you can see, we both look pretty much the same this morning.

NICK: Our point is that you all like Nick because you've known him a long time, but you're snubbing Barry because he's new.

BARRY: Barry does have a face, if you'll take time to see it!

17

NICK: Barry is a pretty nice guy if you'll take time to find out.

BARRY: (Removing his bag.) True, I'm new, but I'll be one of you before long if you'll give me a chance and get to know me! (**NICK** removes his bag, too.)

MIKE: I guess we've been crummy, Barry.

BRANDY: Yeah, we think we're real cute sometimes.

SEAN: I would like to hear more about that state you came from. What did you say it was called?

BARRY: I'll tell you about it at lunch, Sean.

JOE: Let's play Red Rover again at P.E. You and I will be team captains. OK, Barry?

BARRY: Sounds great to me! Thanks!

(All the boys and girls get their "bagheads" and get in place to sing while the **NARRATOR** speaks.)

NARRATOR: (Entering.) This ends the story of Barry Brizenbean, the baghead. The boys and girls forgot that he was new and got to know him, and they liked what they saw. And now, here's the Baghead Choir!

ALL: (Musical score page 11.)

"The Baghead Song"

Don't judge someone by the way that he looks.
You know what they say 'bout the covers of books.
Take time to know him, he might be really nice.
And you wouldn't know if you hadn't looked twice.

If a new girl comes to live in your town
You should get to know her, just sit her right down.
Then you just ask her what she likes to play,
She might turn out to be your best friend some day!

There's something good 'bout most everyone.
Trying to find it can really be fun.
Thank you for coming to see our play.
Now don't treat anyone like a baghead today!

THE SCARY CONTEST

THE CAST

- **Ertha Cat**

- **Pillowcase the Ghost**

- **Jack O' Lantern**

- **T-Bone the Skeleton**

- **Bumpnose the Witch**

- **Terry Tough-Guy**

- **The Principal or The Teacher**

- **Boys and Girls at Terry's Party**

NOTES TO THE TEACHER/DIRECTOR:

The Scary Contest is a short play for Halloween. It is the story of Ertha Cat, Pillowcase the Ghost, Jack O' Lantern, T-Bone the Skeleton, and Bumpnose the Witch. Each thinks he is the scariest Halloween ghoul, so together they stage a contest. They visit Terry Tough-Guy's house (the toughest kid in school) and attempt to frighten the boys and girls at his Halloween party. Terry's guests are not frightened by any of them until the school principal (or classroom teacher) visits his home.

Include as many students as you would like in the Halloween party scene. Terry Tough-Guy has specific lines, but the rest of the lines are designated as boy or girl.

There are a few places to personalize your production. For instance, one of the girls at the party remarks that some pretty strange guests are arriving, and Terry Tough-Guy says that they may be from _____ Elementary School (you should insert the name of a rival elementary school in this line).

Ertha Cat's song is a rap-style song. No music is included because it is more like a chant. Your students can accompany him/her by clapping.

Words or phrases used in this play which may be new to the students include:

ad-lib	eerie	"hold a candle to it"	leprechaun	suggest
confess	expensive	hysterical	offended	terrified
contest	ferocious	implying	strike (in theatrical context)	

The class should become familiar with these words and phrases before beginning work on the play. Teaching materials are included.

PROPS

- Board game
- Broom
- Hand mirror
- Tub of water with apples for bobbing
- Plate of cookies

SCENERY

The first scene takes place in the forest. The easiest way to create the scene is for the students to draw trees on the chalkboard with colored chalk. Then act the scene in front of it. The students should then erase the trees to "strike" the forest scene and move to TERRY'S living room. Schools with a

CUT ART BOARD INTO THE SHAPES YOU WANT

GLUE & PAINT

DRAW ON CHALKBOARD

PAINT ON ART BOARD

larger budget and scenic ambition can use sheets of artboard or a white, paper-covered sheet of foam. The foam creates a stiff sheet which can be leaned against a wall or desk, and the paper covering is suitable for drawing or painting trees.

The second scene takes place in TERRY'S living room. Use desks pushed together and covered with blankets or quilts (to become sofas) and add several cushions or pillows. If students could bring tables or lamps from home, that would, of course, enhance your setting.

You can affix warts made of putty or modeling clay to her nose by using a substance called "spirit gum" which is available at magic stores and costume shops. It is an adhesive which can be applied to the skin without harm. Another fun idea, however, is to cut one egg holder out of a cardboard egg carton, decorate it as you wish, and affix it to her head by a piece of elastic stapled to the sides as a mask.

PILLOWCASE THE GHOST can wear a sheet, trimmed to fit, with eye and mouth holes. The sheet should be a flowered print rather than white.

COSTUMES

BUMPNOSE THE WITCH should wear a long, dark skirt, dark print blouse, and a shawl. An inexpensive witch wig and cone-shaped hat from the drugstore would add to the fun. But, the hat can easily be made out of construction paper and secured with a piece of elastic stapled to each side of the cone. There are several ways to create a "bumpnose." Dot the nose of your actress with an eyebrow pencil, creating a wart-like appearance.

ERTHA CAT should wear black jeans, slacks, bike pants, or leotards and a black turtleneck or sweatshirt. Her ears can be fashioned from construction paper and affixed to her head by hairpins under her hair. Or, affix construction paper ears to a headband. Her whiskers and nose can be painted on with an eyebrow pencil, or make the whiskers from pipe cleaners. For her claws, attach inexpensive, long fake fingernails to an old pair of black gloves and paint the nails gold or an iridescent color. Attach a black belt to her seat for a tail.

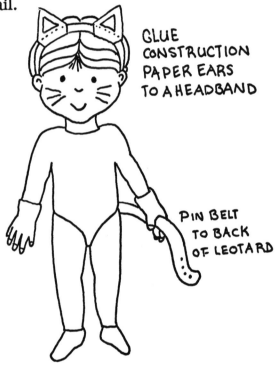

GLUE CONSTRUCTION PAPER EARS TO A HEADBAND

PIN BELT TO BACK OF LEOTARD

T-BONE THE SKELETON can be costumed in a couple of different ways. A drugstore skeleton costume (mask optional) would work just fine. If one is not available, let him wear black clothes which can be painted (old, almost outgrown clothes or black pants and shirt from a thrift store). Then, using white tempera paint, paint a skeleton. You can use white makeup available at magic stores or white cream eyeshadow

for his face. (Of course, all makeup is removable by cold cream.) He can be barefoot, wear white sneakers, or old black sneakers with bones painted on them.

JACK O' LANTERN'S roundness can be created by an illusion. Find a T-shirt several sizes larger than your actor. An orange T-shirt would be ideal. If it has lettering, turn it inside out. Or use an old white T-shirt several sizes too large. Using tempera paints, paint eyes, nose, and mouth on the T-shirt as illustrated.

GIRL SCOUT BERET

BIG ORANGE T-SHIRT

GREEN SHIRT

STUFF SHIRT WITH NEWS- PAPERS & TIE OFF THE BOTTOM

GREEN TIGHTS →

Then, using pillows, scraps from Mom's sewing, or even facial tissue, stuff the T-shirt to make him round. Put pins or ties at the bottom to hold it in, or simply tuck it in your actor's pants. Again, orange or green pants would be ideal but may not be readily available. Jeans or black trousers will do fine. A fun finishing touch would be a small green hat – a green felt beret would be perfect. (Shop thrift stores for an old-style Girl Scout beret.) The tip of the beret will give the illusion of a stem.

TERRY TOUGH-GUY and FRIENDS can either wear regular clothing or Halloween costumes. If you choose regular clothing, it might be fun to dress TERRY in a white T-shirt with the sleeves rolled up and/or a leather jacket to make him look tough. If you use Halloween costumes, make sure no one looks too much like your main characters.

PRINCIPAL/TEACHER is possibly your most challenging character to costume. The student should dress, act, and speak as closely as possible to the adult he is portraying. Obviously, a suit and tie are needed for

a male principal, etc., but be sure to observe details closely and try to match any glasses, etc.

TEACHING MATERIALS:

I. Writing Exercises

T-BONE THE SKELETON is so in love with the letter "T" that he tries to use as many words as he can that begin with "T." Have your students make a list of as many words as they can think of which begin with the letter "T." Let them decide whether or not some of these words could be added to T-BONE'S lines so he can say even more "T" words.

II. After explaining to your class that to ad-lib means to say lines the characters would say that aren't actually written in the script, allow two or three students at a time to ad-lib in front of the class about the following topics:

    A.   A good television show they saw recently.

    B.   What they think of their hometown.

    C.   What they would like to do when they grow up.

    D.   What kind of pet is the best to have and why.

    E.   Other topics your class might choose.

Explain to them that they ad-lib in regular conversation each day, but the difference in a play is that they choose things to say that are consistent with what they know about each character.

THE SCARY CONTEST

A Play for Halloween

(The play begins in the woods on Halloween afternoon. **ERTHA, PILLOWCASE**, and **JACK O' LANTERN** are playing a board game on the ground. **T-BONE** is pacing back and forth in front of them. **BUMPNOSE** is sitting close by polishing her broom.)

JACK: Ha, ha! You crossed over my man! That means ten points for me!

PILLOWCASE: Does that mean I lose?

ERTHA: No, Pillowcase, it doesn't mean you lose. It just means I get an extra turn!

PILLOWCASE: Really, Ertha? OK, here are the dice.

JACK: Pillowcase, don't give her those dice! Don't you know that sneaky Ertha Cat well enough by now to know that she's pulling your sheet?

PILLOWCASE: (Looking at his sheet.) I didn't feel anything!

JACK: It's my turn and I'm going to win this game or my name isn't Jack O' Lantern!

ERTHA: Is that an Irish name, Jack?

JACK: No, it's an I-WISH name. **I wish** you'd hand me the dice and let me roll!

T-BONE: How in the world can the three of you sit still and play a game on the most exciting, thrilling afternoon of the year? I'm too tense!

BUMPNOSE: Don't ask me, T-Bone! There's so much to do to get ready! Because tonight is...

BUMPNOSE and **T-BONE:** Halloween!

BUMPNOSE: Take this broom, for instance. I haven't ridden it in a year! It's bound to be full of splinters! Ouch! That wouldn't be a very smooth ride! Ha, ha, ha! (She laughs a cackling laugh.)

ERTHA: Aw, T-Bone, we're just passing the time! We're very excited, too!

PILLOWCASE: Why are we excited, Ertha?

ERTHA: Because it's Halloween, Pillowcase, my man! The one night of the year when all of us scary types creep out of our secret homes and run around the city scaring everybody out of their wits!

JACK: It's the best!

T-BONE: It sure is! This year I feel tremendously scary!

BUMPNOSE: So do I, T-Bone! I can just see the faces of the boys and girls when I go riding by, cackling...

JACK: And picking out splinters!

PILLOWCASE: Look how scary I can be! Woo, woo! (He runs back and forth waving his arms. The others watch him but do not appear to be afraid. **PILLOWCASE** looks at them.) Oh, I'm sorry, everybody. I didn't mean to make you so hysterical!

JACK: It's OK, Pillowcase. I think we'll calm down here in a minute...

T-BONE: Yep, this is my year! I'm the top spook of all the goblins, and I...

ERTHA: Now wait a minute, my fine bag of bones! Surely you're not implying that you're scarier than I, a ferocious, hissing black cat! Meow! Hiss! (She makes a scratching motion at the air.)

BUMPNOSE: Or me, T-Bone! I'm a mean old witch who can't wait to ride in front of the moon and cast an eerie shadow over the land! Ha, ha, ha! Surely you don't think you can outspook me!

T-BONE: I'm sorry if I've offended you, my fine scary friends! I didn't mean to step on anyone's toes. But, I do confess that I am the scariest one of all!

PILLOWCASE: I'll settle this! (He produces a mirror, looks at himself, and screams as if frightened.) Ahhhh! Nope, I'm the scariest. I even scared myself!

JACK: You're all wrong! Nothing is as scary as a jack o' lantern carved with a wicked grin! I can't wait to frighten boys and girls tonight! You can't hold a candle to me, T-Bone, but you can put one inside me once I'm hollowed out!

ERTHA: Hey, I've got it! We'll have a scary contest!

PILLOWCASE: A scary contest, Ertha?

ERTHA: Sure! There's a Halloween party tonight at Terry Tough-Guy's house.

T-BONE: He's the toughest guy in town!

ERTHA: He sure is, and all his tough buddies will be there bobbing for apples and having fun. I suggest that we go there, one by one, and see which one of us is scariest to the kids!

JACK: What a great idea!

BUMPNOSE: Then we'll know for sure who's the scariest one of all! I'll go first! Come on, everybody!

ALL: Yeah! A scary contest! I'll be the winner! (They ad-lib.)

(They strike the trees and exit. **TERRY TOUGH-GUY** and friends enter. This can be as many students as the teacher/director wishes, but there should be at least five including **TERRY**. The teacher/director should divide the lines among the students at the party. **TERRY** and his group should set up the living room of **TERRY'S** house. Use several chairs pushed together to form a sofa and put a blanket or quilt over them and add several pillows. It might be fun to have an actual bucket with water in it and have several students bobbing for apples. Some boys and girls are dancing.)

A BOY: Hey, Terry Tough-Guy!

TERRY: Hey, dude!

A BOY: How are ya?

TERRY: Tough, dude, I'm feelin' real tough.

A BOY: Not afraid of anything, eh, Terry?

TERRY: Nothing I've seen yet!

A GIRL: Hey, Terry! Come bob for apples with us!

TERRY: Stand back, girls, the world champion apple-bobber is here!

A GIRL: Wow, look at him go!

TERRY: (He sneaks his hand into the water and quickly shoves an apple into his mouth.) Ta da!

A GIRL: What a guy!

TERRY: Hey, I'm the greatest!

(**BUMPNOSE** enters riding her broom.)

BUMPNOSE: Hello, boys and girls, and a Happy Halloween to you! I suppose you know what I am!

(The **BOYS** and **GIRLS** stop what they're doing and stare at her.)

Well, since you're too terrified to speak, I'll tell you! My name if Bumpnose, and I am an honest-to-goodness **witch**! Ha, ha, ha! (She cackles.) Now stand back before I cast a spell on you!

A GIRL: She's cute!

ANOTHER GIRL: She reminds me of my grandmother!

BUMPNOSE: Your grandmother? Cute? But I'm a scary, cackling witch! Aren't you scared?

TERRY: Of a sweet old lady like you? Nahhh!

A BOY: Somebody get her something to eat.

A GIRL: Like some cookies!

A BOY: Do you like oatmeal cookies, ma'am?

BUMPNOSE: Oatmeal?

A GIRL: Yes! Homemade!

BUMPNOSE: Well...maybe one or two...

A BOY: Great! Somebody help her off her broom.

A GIRL: Say, could we borrow that? We spilled popcorn over here and we need to sweep it up.

A BOY: Yeah, Terry's parents hate for us to leave their house in a mess.

BUMPNOSE: Sweep? With my broom?

A GIRL: You don't have to do the sweeping. Just lend it to us and we'll sweep while you eat cookies.

BUMPNOSE: Well, all right.

(The **BOYS** and **GIRLS** lead **BUMPNOSE** to the cookies and she begins eating as **JACK O' LANTERN** enters.)

JACK: Hey, hey, hey, boys and girls! Look who's here! Someone round, someone orange, someone really **scary**!

TERRY: (Looking right and left.) Where?

JACK: Right here! I'm the scariest thing you've ever seen...or my name's not Jack O' Lantern!

A BOY: Is that an Irish name?

JACK: Why does everyone always ask me that? Do I look like a leprechaun?

A GIRL: No, but you really are pretty! I just love pretty, carved jack o' lanterns to put in the window on Halloween.

A BOY: Me, too, and we forgot to get one this year!

A GIRL: The ones at the market were so expensive!

TERRY: What do you say, Jack? Would you like to sit in our window?

JACK: What? You mean you wouldn't be scared to have me in your house?

A BOY: No! We think you look great!

ALL: Yeah! We do! (Ad-libbing.)

JACK: So I could sit in the window and look out?

TERRY: Yes, and all the boys and girls who are out trick-or-treating will see you!

JACK: Hmmm...could be fun.

A GIRL: Come on, Jack. I'll show you to the front window.

(They take **JACK** to the "front window." This can be at the front of the party facing the class. He sits and looks out happily.)

A GIRL: Terry, there are some really strange guests showing up here at your party!

TERRY: I can't tell who they really are in their costumes. Maybe they're from _____ (insert name of rival elementary school).

(**T-BONE** enters.)

T-BONE: Look out, everybody! It's me, T-Bone! I'm terrible, terrifying, and too, too bad!

A GIRL: Now what?

TERRY: I don't know. T-Bone, you look a little skinny.

T-BONE: Of course I'm skinny. I'm a skeleton! Did you ever see a fat skeleton?

TERRY: Well, no...

T-BONE: I will be too glad to teach you how to feel really terrified!

A GIRL: Bad news, T-Bone. We're not afraid of you.

T-BONE: What?

A BOY: We're worried about you, though. It's not good to be **too** skinny. Let's fix him some cookies and milk.

28

TERRY: Yeah, let's get some meat on those bones.

T-BONE: But that's too silly! A skeleton with...did you say cookies and milk?

TERRY: Oatmeal!

T-BONE: Lead the way!

(He joins **BUMPNOSE. PILLOWCASE** enters tripping on his sheet and falling down.)

PILLOWCASE: Oops! I...oops!

A GIRL: Are you all right?

PILLOWCASE: No...I'm scary! Wooo!

A BOY: Are you sure? You don't look scary to me.

PILLOWCASE: Sure! I'm a ghost, and ghosts are scary!

TERRY: Well, friend, let me tell you something. Ghosts with flowered sheets are not quite as scary!

PILLOWCASE: Really? I knew I should've used a solid. And they were on sale at _____ (insert local department store).

A GIRL: Don't worry about it. It really is a pretty sheet. I love _____ flowers. (Insert the color of **PILLOWCASE'S** sheet here.)

ANOTHER GIRL: Yeah! I'd love to have that color in my room.

PILLOWCASE: But, you're not even a little bit scared? Let me see your hands.

(All the **BOYS** and **GIRLS** hold up their hands.)

They're not trembling at all!

TERRY: Don't feel bad! Come over here and join us for...

(**ERTHA** bursts into the room interrupting him. She sings a rap song.)

Hey, hey, my name is Ertha and I'm a rappin' cat.
I'm not a pumpkin and I'm not a bat.
I like to screech and yowl all night
To give you all a mighty fright.
Meow, meow! I said, "Meow!"

I never purr, I don't drink milk.
I don't have fur as soft as silk.
I'm bad to the bone, I'm really mean.
I'm the scariest creature this Halloween!
Meow, meow! I said, "Meow!"

(All the **BOYS** and **GIRLS** cheer and clap their hands.)

TERRY: What a great song!

A BOY: You're the best!

A GIRL: But what a cute little kitty!

A BOY: She really is...do you have a home?

ERTHA: Aw, come on, dude! Aren't you scared of me?

A GIRL: What's going on here? They all want to know if we're scared!

ERTHA: I guess it can't hurt to tell. Bumpnose, T-Bone, Jack O' Lantern, Pillowcase, and I wanted to find out who is the scariest. So we had a little contest to see who could scare you the most.

JACK: That's right, but it looks as if none of us were too scary.

BUMPNOSE: Maybe not, but it sure was nice to be welcomed into this house and invited to stay!

T-BONE: These cookies are great!

PILLOWCASE: (Runs by waving his arms.) Wooo! Is the contest over? Did I win?

TERRY: A scary contest! How funny. Sorry we weren't more scared, but you see, we're really tough kids here. Not too much scares us.

A BOY: Terry's right. I can't think of anybody who could give me a scare.

(The **PRINCIPAL** or the **TEACHER** enters.)

TERRY: It's _____ ! (Insert his/her name.)

(The **BOYS** and **GIRLS** run and hide and cower down looking very frightened.)

PRINCIPAL/TEACHER: Terry? Terry, where are you? I need to speak to your mother Mrs. Tough-Guy about a day you were absent. Terry?

ERTHA: Well, _____ , (insert his/her name) it looks like you win the contest! Ha, ha, ha!

(**ERTHA, T-BONE, JACK, PILLOWCASE,** and **BUMPNOSE** laugh. All the **CAST** turn to the audience and say:)

CAST: Happy Halloween!

SHARING THANKSGIVING

THE CAST

- **Brandon Dickson**
- **Nana** (*Brandon's grandmother*)
- **Mom** (*Pandy Dickson*)
- **Sarah** (*Brandon's cousin*)
- **Dad** (*John Dickson*)
- **Constance** (*a settler from Plymouth Colony*)
- **Nauset**
- **King Massasoit**
- **Governor Carver**
- **Squanto**
- **Indians**
- **Settlers from Plymouth Colony**

NOTES TO THE TEACHER/DIRECTOR:

Sharing Thanksgiving is about the first Thanksgiving at Plymouth Colony in 1621. The story begins when Brandon Dickson, a present-day boy, can't get anyone in his family to listen to the report he has written for school. It is about the first Thanksgiving. He is very proud of the "A" he received. His relatives are anxious to hear all about it – but later, when they are not so involved in preparing Thanksgiving dinner. He retreats to his room and takes a nap during which he is visited by Constance, a pilgrim girl and Nauset, a boy from the Wampanoag Indian tribe. They show him scenes from the first Thanksgiving at Plymouth Colony and tell him what it was really like. They discuss the trip over on the Mayflower; the relationship between the settlers and the Indians of the Wampanoag tribe; and the foods eaten, utensils used, and games played at the first Thanksgiving. He awakens feeling as if he knows more than he did when he wrote his paper. He joins his family for Thanksgiving dinner.

The first seven roles on the cast list are speaking roles, but the actors who play Massasoit, Governor Carver, Squanto, the extra Indians, and the extra settlers act out scenes during Brandon's dream without speaking. Unlimited students may be added to the scene depicting the Indians dancing and the Indians and settlers wrestling. (Girl settlers most likely did not wrestle, but they may have cheered from the sidelines.)

Words used in the play which may be new to your students include:

celebrate	paprika
confused	spoiling (e.g. food spoils)
croquet	treaty
defending	whisk
imagine	

These Indian words are included as well:

Massasoit	samp
sachem	Squanto
sallets	Wampanoag

The class should become familiar with these words before beginning work on the play.

PROPS

- School paper or report
- Whisk
- Several mixing and serving bowls
- Several spoons
- Plates, silverware, glasses, etc., for setting the table
- Peace pipe – use a corncob pipe and decorate it with ribbon, beads, and strips of leather
- Food on the Dickson's table:
  Turkey
  Corn on the cob with butter
  Cranberries
  Dad's beans

Here are some suggestions for providing the above food items. The students could actually bring the food from home. Be sure they do not eat it if it has been sitting out. If you plan to perform the play on the last day before Thanksgiving, many of these items may be on the menu in the school cafeteria and could perhaps be donated. You might also consider making the food items out of cardboard, painting them with tempera paint, and mounting them on small blocks of wood to secure them on the table as illustrated. This will provide a less realistic scene but might be just as much fun because the cast could "make the food" a week before. There's no need to have actual food in the bowls, etc., for the first scene, just provide lots of spoons and make sure the actors pantomime sifting and stirring.

SCENERY

Divide your acting space into three areas:

For the first scene in the kitchen, push several desks together to represent the kitchen counter work area. No covering is really needed because bowls, spoons, and whisks will be on the surface.

After this scene, have the actors leave the desks and strike the props. When the family sits down to Thanksgiving dinner later, cover the same desks with a tablecloth and add chairs to form a dining room area. When BRANDON leaves his bedroom and joins his family at the table, his bedroom stays intact throughout the rest of the play.

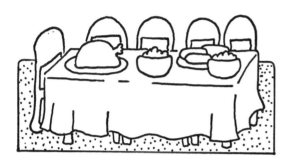

BRANDON'S bedroom can be set up as elaborately as you wish since it does not need to be struck. You can use a cot and make it with sheets and a bedspread, or push desks together and cover them with a spread. Add a basketball or football as well as a jacket and other clothing items. Put a chair in BRANDON'S bedroom so CONSTANCE and NAUSET can sit down occasionally.

The MASSASOIT/SQUANTO/ GOVERNOR CARVER scene and the INDIANS dancing/wrestling scene can take place in the "dream area" while BRANDON and his guests look on from his bedroom. No scenery is needed for this area, but it should be large enough to accommodate all your PILGRIMS and INDIANS in the wrestling scene.

COSTUMES

BRANDON and SARAH should wear jeans, sweaters, etc. NANA should be aged by putting baby powder in her hair. She can also wear a hairnet and/or granny glasses. Let her wear slacks or a more traditional print dress

and an apron. MOM and DAD can dress in at-home holiday attire. MOM might need an apron, too, and it might be fun for DAD to wear a "Kiss the Chef" or some other silly apron since he has cooked his famous beans.

CONSTANCE and your female SETTLERS should wear long dark dresses with white collars and cuffs. Pilgrim girls wore white caps pinned to their hair. The male SETTLERS wore dark knee breeches and dark jackets belted at the waist. They wore knit stockings, buckled shoes, and hats that looked something like this:

The male INDIANS of the Wampanoag tribe wore their hair long, some braided (you might want to experiment with black yarn). A single feather attached to an elastic headband or sweatband will do as a headdress. Since they wore loincloths with bare legs and chests, you might want to alter their costumes and let your braves wear dark pants or shorts, be bare chested, and wear beads around their necks. They wore sandals on their feet.

It would be ideal for someone to sew authentic costumes for the whole cast. If this is not realistic, incorporate these ideas with yours and include dark clothing and aluminum foil-covered buckles, white paper collars, etc.

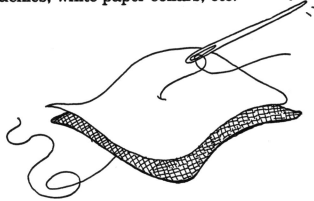

SHARING THANKSGIVING

A Play for Thanksgiving

(The play begins on Thanksgiving Day in the kitchen of the **DICKSON** family. See the **Scenery** page for suggestions for setting up the three acting areas of this play. **NANA** (**BRANDON'S** grandmother), **MOM**, and **BRANDON'S** cousin **SARAH** are busy preparing the Thanksgiving dinner. **BRANDON** excitedly runs in holding a report.)

BRANDON: Nana! Sarah! I have something to tell you!

NANA: Happy Thanksgiving, Brandon! Did you see the parade this morning?

MOM: I love the big balloons, don't you, Nana?

SARAH: I liked the giant turkey! But seeing Santa is always cool.

BRANDON: Yes, the parade was great. But, Mom, I want to tell Sarah and Nana about my Thanksgiving paper!

MOM: Oh, yes! Brandon has been working for a long time on...

BRANDON: (Interrupting.) On a report at school, about...

SARAH: (Interrupting.) Aunt Pandy, will you please pass the paprika? I make great deviled eggs if I do say so myself!

NANA: Sarah, don't interrupt your cousin! What, Brandon?

BRANDON: On a report about the first Thanksgiving and the pilgrims and the Indians! I worked really hard on it, and I made an "A"!

NANA: That's wonderful, Brandon! What exactly did it say?

BRANDON: Well, it...

MOM: (Interrupting.) Excuse me, son, but I need a whisk, please. (**NANA** passes it.) Thanks. The secret to good pumpkin pie is a whisk! Now, go ahead, son.

BRANDON: Well, it was about pumpkin...and turkey...and ears of corn with lots of butter...and all the things they had that first Thanksgiving!

NANA: How interesting!

(**DAD** enters carrying a bowl of beans.)

DAD: Here I am with my famous baked beans! I got up at...

DAD, MOM, NANA, and **SARAH:** At 4 o'clock this morning to start cooking these beans!

(**MOM, NANA,** and **SARAH** laugh. **DAD** looks confused.)

DAD: Have I said that before?

MOM: Every year, John.

NANA: And every year they're delicious. You're a great cook.

BRANDON: So, anyway, do you guys want me to read my paper to you? It would be really interesting...

SARAH: Oh, Brandon, I don't think so...

MOM: Honey, why don't you go lie down for a little while? It's a few hours until we eat, and you could catch a little nap.

NANA: We're really proud of you for making a good grade, but I'm afraid we wouldn't be able to concentrate too well!

BRANDON: Oh, OK. Maybe I'll read it to you after supper?

MOM: That sounds great. Now, bye! Sarah, hand me that big spoon, would you?

(**BRANDON** exits and goes to his room taking his report. The rest of the family exits with their cooking utensils. **BRANDON** lies down on his bed.)

BRANDON: I don't see why they think I should take a nap! I'm not sleepy! It's Thanksgiving Day and I...(his eyes close then snap open) I don't even feel...(his eyes close then snap open again) sleepy at all...(he falls asleep).

(Enter **CONSTANCE**, a pilgrim girl and **NAUSET**, an Indian boy.)

CONSTANCE: Do you think he's asleep?

NAUSET: He must be or we wouldn't be here!

CONSTANCE: He is a handsome boy.

BRANDON: (Hearing them.) Who are you?

NAUSET: Don't be afraid, young Brandon. My name is Nauset, and this is Constance. Constance is from Plymouth Colony. You know it now as Massachusetts.

CONSTANCE: And Nauset is an Indian from the Wam...Wam...

NAUSET: From the Wampanoag tribe. We were great friends to the early settlers at Plymouth Colony.

BRANDON: (Rubbing his eyes.) Am I dreaming?

CONSTANCE: That would be my guess!

BRANDON: But you look so real! I can't believe my eyes!

NAUSET: Happy Thanksgiving!

BRANDON: The same to you!

CONSTANCE: Today is happy, but none could ever be as wonderful as the very first Thanksgiving. The trip over was so hard...

BRANDON: On the Mayflower! I know all about it! I wrote a report!

CONSTANCE: You may not know **all** about it. Did you know that there were many, many of us in a really small space and that we could not bathe or change clothes for thirteen weeks?

BRANDON: My mom hates it if I don't bathe each day!

NAUSET: They had no fresh fruit or vegetables.

BRANDON: I could live without vegetables!

CONSTANCE: I thought so, too, until we sailed. We had to eat meat packed in salty water – we had no other way to keep it from spoiling!

BRANDON: I guess there weren't refrigerators on the Mayflower, huh?

NAUSET: Constance told me that they had to eat hard biscuits. They would dip them in soup to make them soft enough to chew.

BRANDON: Wow...

CONSTANCE: It was very hard, but we wanted to come to America. We wanted to be able to practice whatever religion we chose!

BRANDON: That's still important today.

NAUSET: Thanks to the pilgrims who started it all.

CONSTANCE: Nauset is a good friend. But the best friend we had was an Indian named Squanto.

NAUSET: That was a nickname. His real name was too long for the white man to pronounce. They were used to short names like "John" and "Miles."

CONSTANCE: So we called him Squanto. He spoke English.

BRANDON: Because he studied it in school?

CONSTANCE: No, silly. Because he met some English fishermen and learned from them. He taught us how to fish, how to dry out food so it could be eaten later, and how to grow squash and corn!

NAUSET: Squanto was a great man. He helped work out a "treaty" between the settlers and colonists and Massasoit, the great chief of our tribe.

CONSTANCE: Do you know what a treaty is, Brandon?

BRANDON: It's an agreement to live in peace.

CONSTANCE: That's right.

NAUSET: Look! There they are now.

(**SQUANTO, GOVERNOR CARVER,** and **MASSASOIT** enter the dream area. **CARVER** and **MASSASOIT** sit on the floor facing one another. **SQUANTO** sits beside them and hands **MASSASOIT** a peace pipe which he smokes and then hands to **CARVER.** While the two men are smoking, **BRANDON** and his visitors speak.)

BRANDON: Wow! I get to see!

NAUSET: You dream well, Master Brandon.

BRANDON: So that's Squanto...and Massasoit, right? Who's the other guy?

CONSTANCE: Governor Carver, the first governor of Plymouth Colony. We elected him, but I am sorry to say he died soon after the Mayflower left to return to England.

NAUSET: Then they elected good Governor Bradford who was only 31 years old!

BRANDON: That seems pretty old to me!

NAUSET: Yes, I suppose...

(When **SQUANTO** and **GOVERNOR CARVER** are through smoking the pipe, they stand, embrace, then exit.)

BRANDON: Too bad Squanto isn't alive today! We could use him to help make peace in the world. So tell me more about the first Thanksgiving!

CONSTANCE: Well, we didn't realize we were starting a holiday! We were just happy because we made it through a long, hard winter in America. With the help of the Indians, we had a good harvest and were ready to celebrate!

NAUSET: We Indians already had a celebration called the "Green Corn Dance" each fall, so we were very happy when Governor Bradford invited Chief Massasoit to the settlers' feast.

CONSTANCE: He arrived with ninety braves! We couldn't believe it!

NAUSET: Massasoit, our sachem...

CONSTANCE: That means "chief."

NAUSET: He realized that the pilgrims didn't have enough to feed us, so we went into the woods and killed five deer and brought them to the feast.

CONSTANCE: And what a feast! It lasted three days.

NAUSET: The Indian braves slept in the field each night.

BRANDON: How great! But did you really eat for three days?

NAUSET: No, we had lots of activities. We danced.

(Several **INDIANS** enter and begin to dance.)

BRANDON: What wild dances!

NAUSET: We also wrestled with the settlers.

(Enter some male **SETTLERS** who wrestle in a friendly manner with the **INDIANS**. Then they exit arm in arm.)

CONSTANCE: Then we had a display of weapons.

NAUSET: We Indians shot bows and arrows.

CONSTANCE: And Miles Standish, the settler in charge of defending us, shot off many guns and our cannon.

NAUSET: It was fun to see all the weapons, but it also reminded us how lucky we were to be friends with the white man.

CONSTANCE: We also taught the Indians how to play "stoolball."

BRANDON: Stoolball? Did you sit on stools?

NAUSET: No, silly! It was really fun. We learned to bat a ball through a series of wickets – like your croquet, only rougher.

BRANDON: We still play a sport on Thanksgiving – football – but not for three days! My mom would go crazy!

CONSTANCE: Speaking of your mother...look!

(**MOM** and **NANA** are covering the kitchen table with a tablecloth and setting the table. As **BRANDON** and his visitors talk, the family finishes setting the table, and they all sit down and pantomime eating. See **Props** for suggestions about the food. They are talking happily.)

BRANDON: Hey, it's my family sitting down to Thanksgiving dinner. I'd better join them!

NAUSET: You can't join them yet, you're still asleep! Let's go see what they're having!

(They go over and stand behind the family.)

CONSTANCE: Look, Nauset, turkey is the only meat!

BRANDON: It was the only meat at the first Thanksgiving! That's why we have it!

CONSTANCE: I'm afraid it wasn't! We also had venison or deer meat, ducks, partridges, geese, and lots of seafood!

BRANDON: Seafood? On Thanksgiving? I can go to a seafood restaurant any old day!

NAUSET: We did have lobster! We Indians taught the settlers how to fish out of Cape Cod Bay. They caught shellfish – like crabs and oysters, even eels!

BRANDON: Yuck! Eels!

CONSTANCE: They tasted just like chicken.

NAUSET: Look, they, too, are eating corn!

CONSTANCE: We had a harvest of twenty acres of corn, thanks to the Indians!

NAUSET: The English barley and peas they brought with them didn't make it.

CONSTANCE: So we had hominy...

NAUSET: "Samp," we called it.

CONSTANCE: "Hasty pudding," made of boiled corn, we even fried it into little cakes.

NAUSET: The most fun we had with the settlers, though, was teaching them that if they got the kernels of corn really hot...

BRANDON: You taught them about **popcorn**?

NAUSET: Yes!

BRANDON: You didn't have popcorn in England? How did you watch movies?

CONSTANCE: (Laughing.) We didn't. Oh, look, they're putting something yellow on their corn.

BRANDON: Well, that's butter. Don't tell me you ate corn without butter.

NAUSET: It's true. They didn't bring any cows with them on the Mayflower. No cows, no milk, no butter.

BRANDON: Wow.

CONSTANCE: We had good things, though! Gooseberries...

BRANDON: Gooseberries?

CONSTANCE: Yes, and plums and strawberries. The Indians taught us how to dry cherries. We ate them dried, but we also cooked them in what we called little "dough cases."

BRANDON: Which became "pies" later on, I'll bet!

CONSTANCE: Now you're catching on!

NAUSET: What's that bowl with lots of different things in it?

BRANDON: Where? Oh, that's a salad.

CONSTANCE: Salad...salad...or, "sallet"! The Indians used the word "sallet" to mean parsnips, carrots, turnips, onions...

NAUSET: Cucumbers, radishes, beets, cabbage...

BRANDON: Sort of like vegetables today. You called them "sallets." I wonder if that's where we got the word "salad"?

CONSTANCE: No doubt!

BRANDON: Look, there are my dad's beans. He makes them every year.

NAUSET: Your father cooks? But he's a man!

CONSTANCE: No men cooked in Plymouth Colony. It was women's work! And it was really hard that first Thanksgiving because there were 90 Indian braves, 50 pilgrims, and only **4** women and **2** girls to do all the cooking.

BRANDON: I guess things really have changed!

CONSTANCE: For the better, I'd say!

NAUSET: Look, Constance. Each person has his own plate!

CONSTANCE: How unusual! There were at least two to a plate in our day.

NAUSET: And the plates were wooden.

CONSTANCE: Yes, and we had a few spoons, but none of those little things that look sharp.

BRANDON: You had no forks?

NAUSET: No, we ate with our fingers a great deal.

CONSTANCE: But we did have napkins!

BRANDON: Cool!

CONSTANCE: I see cranberries at your table, too, Brandon. We didn't actually have cranberries to eat until later.

BRANDON: This is so interesting! My paper wasn't so correct after all!

NAUSET: Well, Brandon, it's been great fun. We really need to be going and let you eat your dinner.

BRANDON: Won't you join us?

CONSTANCE: No, we can't! We're just part of your dream. Now, come on back to bed so you can wake up.

(They lead **BRANDON** back to his bed and tuck him in.)

NAUSET: Good-bye, Brandon. Happy Thanksgiving!

CONSTANCE: You know, it doesn't really matter if you eat exactly the same foods we did or whether you play football instead of stoolball.

NAUSET: The point is that the pilgrims started something that has continued all this time. They were brave to come to America, and they celebrated living through a hard winter.

CONSTANCE: As Governor Bradford said, "As one small candle may light a thousand, so the light kindled here has shone unto many."

NAUSET: Close your eyes, young Brandon. Enjoy your day of feasting with your family.

(**BRANDON** closes his eyes briefly, and **NAUSET** and **CONSTANCE** exit.)

BRANDON: Say, guys! Constance? Nauset? (He shakes his head.) I feel like Ebeneezer Scrooge! Hey, Mom! (Getting out of bed and going to the table.) Hey, the weirdest thing...

MOM: There you are, sleepy head!

NANA: We were about to start without you!

DAD: But I knew you'd want to be the first to sample my beans!

BRANDON: I would, Dad, I sure would.

SARAH: Brandon, I hope I didn't hurt your feelings about your paper earlier. I really would like to know more about the first Thanksgiving.

BRANDON: Well, Sarah, I'll talk to you later. It seems I know more about it now than I did when I wrote my paper.

MOM: What?

BRANDON: Never mind. Happy Thanksgiving to you all.

CAST: (Looking out.) Happy Thanksgiving to you!

A GRAND CHRISTMAS

NOTES TO THE TEACHER/DIRECTOR:

Poor Jennifer and Donna! For the first time, they will not spend Christmas with their grandparents because Jennifer and Donna have moved too far away. Their loyal (and somewhat magical) pets and toys overhear them talking about how they'd like Grandma and Grandpa at their house for "a grand Christmas." The pets and toys invoke all the Christmas magic they can muster and transport themselves to the North Pole where they confer with Santa. He fears that he can't help them but then manages to slip airplane tickets into Grandma and Grandpa's stockings. A joyous Christmas morning reunion follows.

A Grand Christmas is perhaps the most challenging "special play" because of the number of students requiring costumes. (See the description of costumes on the following page.) There are fifteen speaking roles, and additional elves may be added to the North Pole scene. The elves' lines are designated "an elf" and "another elf" but may be distributed among more than two elf actors if desired. *A Grand Christmas* should be one of the most interesting plays visually, and since more students get an opportunity to speak than some of the others, it might be a good choice for a public (or at least parental) performance.

Words used in the play which may be new to your students include:

accidentally	dazed	forgotten	upset
collapse	delivered	interrupt	
create	especially	mystery	

The class should become familiar with these words before beginning work on the play. Additional teaching materials are included.

PROPS

- Coloring book
- Crayons
- Piggy bank
- 35 cents
- Phone
- Opened presents including:
    Female barbie doll
    Male barbie doll
    Transformer
    Sweaters
    Socks

SCENERY

The first scene takes place in the girls' bedroom. It can be a cot or some desks pushed together and covered with a bedspread. There is reference to a toy chest; see if a student can bring one from home. HARRY needs a cage. Use a large box and cut slits for a cage-like look. Shred newspapers in the bottom.

An artistic student can create a "running wheel" out of cardboard. If a large box cannot be found, use art board or foam board. (See *The Scary Contest* for details about this art supply.) Make only the front side of the cage and cut holes. Have HARRY get behind it when he needs to be inside.

The second scene in SANTA'S workshop can be very simple. Push desks together to form a large flat worktable surface. A green or red tablecloth covering will add the Christmas touch. Students could bring wreaths and sleigh bells to decorate. Remember, all the decorations must be struck for the living room scene.

The living room should have a sofa or two or three desks pushed together covered with a quilt and/or pillows. A small decorated Christmas tree would be a fun touch. Scatter opened presents listed in the props list and any additional props your students would like to gather such as DAD'S aftershave, MOM'S slippers, etc.

COSTUMES

JENNIFER and DONNA need regular girl clothes in the first scene. A Christmas sweatshirt would be fun. For the living room scene they should wear robes which could be slipped right over their other costumes.

MOM and DAD need robes, and MOM needs slippers, either on her feet or in a box. They could wear glasses, and DAD could carry a pipe. Maybe MOM could wear a hairnet to bed.

GRANDMA and GRANDPA should be dressed in traveling clothes such as coats, hats, and mittens. Make your actors look older and white-headed with baby powder. If students want to experiment with age makeup, use light eyebrow pencils (or real theatrical makeup, if available). Have them "scrunch" their faces and see where their natural wrinkles would be. Then fill in those places with light brown or gray pencils.

RAGGEDY ANN and ANDY'S costumes will, of course, be more involved. Wigs should be fashioned out of bright red yarn. Use a bathing cap to attach the yarn. If an ambitious mom sewed a whole costume using the actual dolls as references, it would be ideal. If this is not possible, use makeup. They need red triangles painted over their noses in red lipstick and the following lines extending from the corners of their mouths using black eye pencil.

Draw eyelashes at the top and bottom of their eyes:

Next, make sure each has red and white striped socks. If these are not available, wind stripes of red masking tape around white knee socks. They should wear black shoes.

RAGGEDY ANN'S dress should be a print, preferably blue and white, and she should wear a white apron. ANDY should wear short blue pants and suspenders, preferably blue with white buttons. ANDY'S shirt should be a blue and white print, blue and white striped, or solid white.

CUDDLES THE BEAR can wear a rented bear outfit or brown pants and a brown shirt or turtleneck sweater. Give him an eyebrow pencil nose and whiskers. Maybe someone could sew a head covering out of brown fake fur or corduroy and attach ears to it. Give him brown mitten paws, or put brown socks on his hands.

draw on features

with eye-brow pencil & rouge

you may attach ears to a brown jacket with a hood

FLUFFY THE PUPPY – If CUDDLES is brown, try making FLUFFY black and white – a white shirt or turtleneck sweater, white pants and black shoes, and mittens and ears, for instance.

To make the ears, get a headband (the rigid plastic kind) and attach floppy pieces of fabric, vinyl, or even construction paper on the sides. Be sure to draw FLUFFY a nose and whiskers, and maybe give him a dog collar as well.

MARY ANN is a beautiful doll. She can be a ballerina or a baby doll with a bottle and "Mary Jane" shoes. Be sure to make her face vivid with rouged cheeks, pink lips, and bold eyelashes.

HARRY HAMSTER and WRIGLEY THE KITTY should be similar to CUDDLES and FLUFFY. HARRY, like CUDDLES, may be brown, but minimize confusion by having this actor move in nervous little jerky motions like a hamster. WRIGLEY can be a black cat if you like. See ERTHA CAT in *The Scary Contest*. Be sure to draw nose and whiskers on both of these characters.

THE ELVES can wear solid red, such as a red turtleneck and red slacks (probably more likely to be available for girl elves), solid green, or a combination. For a younger cast, some red or green pajamas might be elf-like. Helpful parents could help out by sewing simple triangular caps, reminiscent of stocking caps, out of red or green flannel with jingle bells attached to the tip. (Jingle bells could be sewn at random on the whole costume for a festive touch.) Red or green socks should work in lieu of elfin boots.

you may find sweat-suits in red and green

jingle bells

SANTA CLAUS needs, of course, a jolly red and white suit. Usually, one can be borrowed. (You might want to consider casting a male adult, such as a principal or P.E. teacher, in the part of SANTA as a fun touch, and as a more likely candidate to fit the suit!) If you borrow a suit, it will likely come complete with a beard, hat, boots, etc. If one is not available or you want to cast a student and he just can't fit the adult suit, try this: SANTA is working hard, so he just might not be in full uniform. Let him wear a red flannel nightshirt.

A red long underwear style shirt or the top of some thermal underwear, suspenders, and black trousers should suffice. Be sure to give him a full white beard, available from a costume store, or make one out of cotton and attach it to pipe cleaners which hook around the ears. Or give SANTA some wire-rimmed glasses, and attach the cotton to the glasses right in front of the ears.

TEACHING MATERIALS:

I. Writing Exercise

Have your students think about Christmases gone by. Ask them to write a half-page paper about a Christmas when something really magical happened to them (like a gift they received that they didn't expect, a gift they gave that was well-received, a special way of observing the holiday, etc.). Tell them not to put their names on their papers. When they're through, exchange papers and have them read each other's aloud. Ask the class members to try and guess who wrote which paper.

II. Another Writing Exercise

After explaining to the class that dialogue is a conversation between two or more people, have them write a brief dialogue that they feel might take place between some of their toys when they're not at home. Which toys would be the most likely to speak? What would they say to each other? For fun, have the students take the roles of each other's toys, and read a few dialogues.

Words by Judy Truesdell Mecca

"A Grand Christmas"

Music by Jenifer Truesdell Christman and Woody Christman

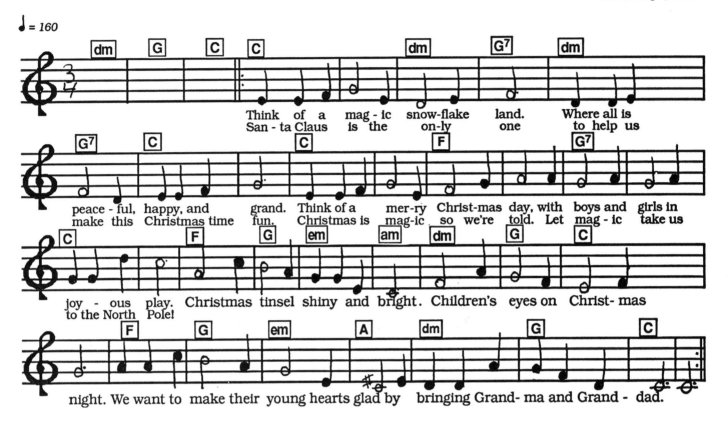

Think of a mag - ic snow-flake land. Where all is
San - ta Claus is the on-ly one to help us

peace - ful, happy, and grand. Think of a mer-ry Christ-mas day, with boys and girls in
make this Christmas time fun. Christmas is mag-ic so we're told. Let mag - ic take us

joy - ous play. Christmas tinsel shiny and bright. Children's eyes on Christ- mas
to the North Pole!

night. We want to make their young hearts glad by bringing Grand- ma and Grand - dad.

Words by Judy Truesdell Mecca

"Christmas Is Magic"

Music by Jenifer Truesdell Christman and Woody Christman

Mag - ic, Christmas is magic, It's a snowy, glowy time of year. Time to hug your fam- i-ly,

ev' ery one that you can see, And to let them know how much you care. Mag - ic, Christmas is magic,

So keep a se - cret smile in - side. Then you'll warm each other, Mother, sis - ter, Dad, and brother with a

Christmas glow you can - not hide.

A GRAND CHRISTMAS

A Play for the Christmas Season

(The play begins the day before Christmas Eve in **JENNIFER** and **DONNA'S** room. Huddled together talking are the toys, **RAGGEDY ANN, RAGGEDY ANDY, CUDDLES THE BEAR, FLUFFY THE PUPPY,** and **MARY ANN**. Real pets **HARRY THE HAMSTER** and **WRIGLEY KITTY** join in as well. They are sitting on the bed, standing, sitting on the floor, and sitting on chairs.)

CUDDLES: I'm so excited that it's almost Christmas again!

RAGGEDY ANN: I can't believe a whole year has gone by since Santa brought me to Jennifer.

RAGGEDY ANDY: And since he brought me to Donna! It's been a great year.

MARY ANN: It's been wonderful having you new toys here with us...only I guess you're not so new anymore, are you?

RAGGEDY ANN: It really feels like we've lived here all our lives.

RAGGEDY ANDY: Yes, it really feels like home here with you toys, Harry Hamster, and Wrigley Kitty!

FLUFFY: Ruff, ruff!

WRIGLEY: It's OK, Fluffy. You can talk! No people are here right now.

FLUFFY: Oh, I forgot!

HARRY: It's better for you to accidentally bark in front of us than to accidentally talk in front of them!

ALL: (Ad-libbing.) Yes! I'll say! For sure!

CUDDLES: Isn't it funny that they still think we can't talk...

MARY ANN: Or walk!

RAGGEDY ANN: I wonder what they think! Why do they think they put us in one place...

RAGGEDY ANDY: Or their mother puts us in one place...

RAGGEDY ANN: Like the toy chest, for instance...

RAGGEDY ANDY: And when they come back, we're someplace else!

FLUFFY: I guess they just blame it on each other!

WRIGLEY: Or they think we **live** pets carry you toys around.

HARRY: I guess.

CUDDLES: As I was saying, I'm so glad it's almost Christmas!

MARY ANN: Just two more days until Christmas morning! What new toys do you think will be joining us?

FLUFFY: I heard Donna asking for another doll.

RAGGEDY ANN: It would be fun if another doll moved in. Then we'd have more clothes to share!

RAGGEDY ANDY: You girl dolls, always thinking about clothes. I hope they get some robots, or...

WRIGLEY: (Interrupting him.) Shh! Listen! I hear them coming!

(The toys freeze. **WRIGLEY** curls up on the floor and pretends to sleep. **HARRY** hurries into his cage and shuts the door. **JENNIFER** and **DONNA** enter.)

JENNIFER: This is the longest day of the year!

DONNA: We get to make one last shopping trip tonight, but what will we do in the meantime? It's not even time to eat supper yet.

JENNIFER: Let's color.

DONNA: OK. (She gets out coloring books and crayons. They color for a minute.)

JENNIFER: It's almost Christmas!

DONNA: I can't wait! I can't wait!

(They jump up, and holding hands, they dance around in a circle saying, "I can't wait, I can't wait!" Then they collapse on the floor giggling.)

JENNIFER: Do you think Santa will bring us the bikes we asked for?

DONNA: Do you think we've been good?

JENNIFER: I think **I've** been good.

DONNA: I think I have, too, but what if Santa thinks you should be **really**, **REALLY** good?

JENNIFER: (Becoming upset.) You mean like what if we had to eat all our carrots all year in order to get a bike?

DONNA: Or what if we have to make all "A's" at school?

JENNIFER: Or help our mother a whole bunch?

JENNIFER and **DONNA: We haven't been good enough!**

(They pretend to faint on the floor or bed.)

DONNA: Now, wait, let's calm down. We haven't gotten in trouble at school...

JENNIFER: We've gotten good grades...

DONNA: Not all "A's," but good grades...

JENNIFER: We make our beds each morning.

DONNA: And help Mom with the laundry every weekend.

JENNIFER and **DONNA: We're OK!**

DONNA: Two more days...

JENNIFER: Till Christmas!

JENNIFER and **DONNA:** Yea! Yea!

(They get up and dance around in a circle again and fall down. While the girls are spinning, **RAGGEDY ANN** turns to a toy near her and says:)

RAGGEDY ANN: I'm afraid they're going to hurt themselves if Christmas doesn't get here soon!

THE OTHER TOY: Shh!

(They look to make sure the girls haven't seen them talking. They haven't.)

DONNA: You know what makes me a little sad?

JENNIFER: Yes, I do.

JENNIFER and **DONNA:** Grandma and Grandpa.

DONNA: It's not fair we had to move so far away from them.

JENNIFER: We've spent Christmas with them every year, and now we won't get to see them at all.

DONNA: It really is sad. I wish we had a million dollars so we could send them airplane tickets!

JENNIFER: So do I. But we'll call them long distance...

DONNA: It won't be the same.

JENNIFER: They sent us a present...

DONNA: It won't be the same.

JENNIFER: No.

MOM: (From offstage.) Girls! Come and help me set the table!

DONNA: Aw, Mom, we're coloring...

JENNIFER: Wait, Donna...**bicycles**!

DONNA: We'd love to, Mother!

JENNIFER: We'll be right down!

(They exit, and the toys and pets come back to life.)

CUDDLES: I've never seen them like that!

RAGGEDY ANDY: Excited one minute, sad the next...girls!

FLUFFY: I wish we could do something to help them.

HARRY: Yes. I know how much they miss their grandparents.

WRIGLEY: They're really nice grandparents. Grandma is especially fond of cats and always brings me a catnip toy.

RAGGEDY ANN: They really are nice.

MARY ANN: What could we do to help get them here?

RAGGEDY ANDY: Look in Jennifer and Donna's piggy bank. Maybe they have enough for an airplane ticket and they just forgot!

CUDDLES: You look, Mary Ann! You have fingers!

MARY ANN: All right. (She goes and gets the piggy bank and spills out its contents. The toys and pets all count together.)

ALL: 5, 10, 15, 20, 25, 30, 35 cents.

HARRY: Will that do it?

RAGGEDY ANDY: I don't know. Let's call someone and ask.

RAGGEDY ANN: I'll make sure no one's on the phone.

(She lifts the receiver carefully and gives the "OK sign" to the others.)

I'll call the operator! She knows everything!

(She dials "0.")

Hello, operator? Can you get a plane ticket for 35 cents? (To the others.) She's laughing. I guess that means "no."

(She hangs up.)

CUDDLES: Well, what can we do?

WRIGLEY: There's only one person I can think of who can help us.

FLUFFY: Who's that, Wrigley?

CUDDLES: I think I know.

HARRY: Is he round and fat?

MARY ANN: Does he say, "Ho, ho, ho?"

RAGGEDY ANN: Did he bring almost all of us to this house on Christmas?

RAGGEDY ANDY: Does he live at the North Pole?

WRIGLEY: Yes!

ALL: SANTA CLAUS!

FLUFFY: But how can we talk to him? He's too busy this time of the year to answer the phone. It just rings and rings.

CUDDLES: No, we can't call him.

MARY ANN: You know, Christmas is a magical time of year...

RAGGEDY ANDY: And we're already magical toys and animals or we wouldn't be able to talk and walk and be so brilliant.

(They all rub their fingers on their shirts in a humble, yet proud manner.)

RAGGEDY ANN: I know what you're thinking, Andy. Maybe we could use a little Christmas magic to get us to the North Pole to talk to Santa!

HARRY: Do you think?

MARY ANN: It's worth a try!

WRIGLEY: But how?

RAGGEDY ANN: I don't know for sure. But it makes sense that if we all hold hands...

(**HARRY** clears his throat.)

RAGGEDY ANN: And paws!
(They form a line, all holding hands.)

RAGGEDY ANN: And sing about the nicest Christmas things we know, we just might create a little magic!

ALL: (Musical score page 50.)

"A Grand Christmas"

Think of a magic snowflake land.
Where all is peaceful, happy, and grand.
Think of a merry Christmas Day,
With boys and girls in joyous play.

Santa Claus is the only one
To help us make this Christmastime fun.
Christmas is magic so we're told.
Let Christmas magic take us to the North Pole!

Christmas tinsel shiny and bright.
Children's eyes on Christmas night.
We want to make their young hearts glad
By bringing Grandma and Granddad.

Christmas tinsel shiny and bright.
Children's eyes on Christmas night.
We want to make their young hearts glad
By bringing Grandma and Granddad.

(Still holding hands, they form a circle and spin around and around. While they twirl, **SANTA'S ELVES** strike the bedroom set and set up desks to form **SANTA'S** workshop. When it's set, the toys and pets drop hands and look around dazed, as if unable to believe they're really at the North Pole.)

CUDDLES: We made it!

FLUFFY: We're really here!

RAGGEDY ANN: The magic worked!

AN ELF: Say, what are you toys doing unwrapped?

ANOTHER ELF: We've been working hard day and night trying to get you all ready, and you're not helping!

MARY ANN: Wait, Mr. Elf, you don't understand. We already belong to Jennifer and Donna.

RAGGEDY ANDY: You delivered us several years ago.

FLUFFY: We're here because Jennifer and Donna are sad.

HARRY: And they need our help!

AN ELF: (Looking at **HARRY**.) Say, we do better work than I thought! You and the kitty look real!

WRIGLEY: Well, we **are** real. You see...

RAGGEDY ANN: Never mind that. We need to see Santa Claus **now**!

AN ELF: Santa Claus? You must be kidding!

ANOTHER ELF: On December 23rd? Not a chance.

FLUFFY: Don't you remember Donna and Jennifer? They're very nice girls. They were so happy the year you left Raggedy Ann and Andy under the tree.

RAGGEDY ANDY: Don't forget how pleased they were to get you, Fluffy! And Cuddles the Bear! They've been good all year...

AN ELF: So what do you want? They're getting their bikes!

MARY ANN: They need more than bikes this year. They need their grandparents.

ANOTHER ELF: What is this, "Confuse an elf day"? Will somebody tell me what's going on?

WRIGLEY: They had to move far away from their grandparents, and they won't get to spend Christmas together!

AN ELF: That **is** sad!

CUDDLES: So, may we please speak to Santa? Just for a minute?

AN ELF: I'll go see what I can do.

(**SANTA** enters.)

SANTA: Do about what?

(All the animals and toys ad-lib and talk at once saying hello to **SANTA** and talking about **JENNIFER** and **DONNA** and their problem.

SANTA: Hold on, hold on! Ho, ho, ho! One at a time! Now what's the problem? Surely you don't want me to take you to different homes?

RAGGEDY ANN: Heavens no, Santa! We love Jennifer and Donna very much.

RAGGEDY ANDY: But we need your help getting their grandparents to them.

SANTA: Oh yes, I remember getting a letter from the girls. Something about airplane tickets...or was it one million dollars?

MARY ANN: Is it too late to help them, Santa?

SANTA: Now, my friends, listen to me. I can make blocks and dolls and choo-choo trains. I can make books and robots and video games. I can even send magical hamsters and cats that talk when the people are gone. But airplane tickets are not something I can make!

WRIGLEY: But, Santa, you have Christmas magic in your fingertips!

SANTA: Yes, Wrigley Kitty. But there are some problems even magic can't solve.

(The toys and pets look very sad and turn to leave.)

SANTA: All I can tell you is I'll do my very Santa-Claus-Christmas-Magic best. Is that a deal?

RAGGEDY ANN: That's a great deal, Santa!

SANTA: Now, "give me five" and scoot back to your house before they notice you're gone!

(The toys and pets ad-lib "thank-you's" to Santa. They then hold hands in a circle again. While they twirl around, **SANTA'S ELVES** strike the workshop and set up the living room in **JENNIFER** and **DONNA'S** house. There should be many opened presents, lots of sweaters and socks, barbie dolls, and a robot. **JENNIFER** and **DONNA** are in their robes sitting on the floor looking almost happy. **MOM** and **DAD**, also in robes, are on the sofa. The toys and pets are scattered around the room. The toys freeze; the animals act like normal, "nonmagical" animals. **HARRY THE HAMSTER** hides behind the sofa so he won't be discovered and sent back to his cage.)

JENNIFER: Mom and Dad, it was the greatest Christmas morning ever!

DONNA: Thanks so much for all the gifts! I can't wait to ride my new bike.

JENNIFER: Santa was really tricky leaving them outside! I thought he had forgotten!

MOM: Yes, Santa can be tricky sometimes.

DAD: Thank you, girls, for my aftershave! It's my favorite.

JENNIFER and **DONNA:** You're welcome.

MOM: And I love my slippers. They're really warm.

DONNA: It was a great Christmas morning.

JENNIFER: I only wish...

DONNA: Jennifer, don't say it.

MOM: You only wish that your grandparents could be with us?

DAD: It's OK to say it. We miss them, too.

MOM: But you can bet they're having a Merry Christmas, too, and...

(**GRANDMA** and **GRANDPA** wearing hats and mittens have entered quietly behind the family.)

GRANDMA: You bet we are!

JENNIFER and **DONNA:** Grandma! Grandpa!

(They all jump up and hug **GRANDMA** and **GRANDPA**.)

MOM: I'm so glad to see you! How did you manage to get here?

GRANDMA: You mean you don't know?

DAD: Don't know what?

GRANDPA: As you know, Grandma and I still hang our stockings on the mantle. Well, last night when we looked in them, we saw airline tickets! We were sure you sent them!

GRANDMA: But we wondered how in the world you put them in our stockings!

MOM: We didn't, Mother! What a mystery!

DAD: Must've been good old Santa!

GRANDPA: There **were** footprints in the snow out by the chimney...

JENNIFER and **DONNA:** Christmas magic!

GRANDMA: Anyway, we took the first flight out this morning, and here we are!

MOM: We're so glad you are!

(As they all hug, the magical toys and pets come to the front of the stage.)

CUDDLES: It was Christmas magic!

FLUFFY: We did it!

(They give each other "high fives." **SANTA** and **THE ELVES** come out. **GRANDMA, GRANDPA, MOM, DAD, JENNIFER,** and **DONNA** all join the others at the front of the stage where the whole cast sings.)

ALL: (Musical score page 50.)

"Christmas is Magic"

Magic, Christmas is magic,
It's a snowy, glowy time of year.
Time to hug your family,
Everyone that you can see,
And let them know how much you care.

Magic, Christmas is magic,
So keep a secret smile inside.
Then you'll warm each other,
Mother, sister, dad, and brother,
With a Christmas glow you cannot hide.

RAGGEDY ANN: Keep the magic of Christmas, everyone!

ALL: Merry Christmas!

(The **CAST** waves to the audience.)

THE SCHOOL FOR CUPIDS

THE CAST

- **Ms. Lovejoy** (*the teacher*)
- **Hardy**
- **Sunny**
- **Hope**

(*Other students if you like*)

- **Ms. Johnson**
- **Joe Johnson**
- **Paul Johnson**
- **Mr. McCoy**
- **Mrs. McCoy**
- **Elaine**
- **Elise**
- **Janet**
- **Jim**

NOTES TO THE TEACHER/DIRECTOR:

The School for Cupids is a play with several messages. Hardy, Sunny, and Hope are three students taking Cupid lessons from their teacher Ms. Lovejoy. She takes them to the park to demonstrate the art of spreading love throughout the world. Ms. Lovejoy overhears Ms. Johnson and her two sons speaking about a problem, and she helps them negotiate a peaceful settlement. Ms. Lovejoy demonstrates it is possible to remind people of the love in their hearts. She sends her students out on their own to do the same. Each student encounters people in need of help, and each would-be Cupid helps bring love into their lives. At the end of the play, the Cupids receive their wings.

The main theme is that all of us can spread love in the world. There are two other messages included in *The School for Cupids* – the importance of compromise in relationships and the importance of communication.

This play requires little in terms of costumes and scenery. The only real challenge is the construction of wings for the Cupids. This play is, however, one of the more challenging in terms of acting and dialogue, but your students should find it well worth any extra effort. The messages are important, and the story is an enjoyable and entertaining one.

The number of Cupid students can be expanded as needed, though only three have lines. Other Cupids can be added in the beginning scene and at the end for the wing awards and the song.

Words or phrases in the play which may be new to your students include:

aside	budget	full-fledged	remained
(theatrical context)	confused	"I'm all ears"	suggestion
bored	eager	overhearing	

The class should become familiar with these words and phrases before beginning work on the play. Additional teaching materials are included.

62

PROPS

- Purse
- Envelope with love dust (red glitter, confetti, or sequins)
- Knitting needles and yarn
- Newspaper

SCENERY

The first scene takes place in a classroom of the School for Cupids. Provide a "teacher's desk" for MS. LOVEJOY, and arrange desks in the acting area to accommodate the number of CUPIDS (at least three). Write "School for Cupids" on the chalkboard.

The rest of the play takes place in the park. Rearrange the desks to be park benches – two or three on each side of the acting area facing the audience. (Chairs without writing surfaces will work best.) Have CUPIDS erase the board and draw trees, sun, birds, etc., as time allows.

COSTUMES

MS. LOVEJOY should wear a red dress or a red skirt and blouse. The CUPID students should dress in solid red or solid pink if possible. If not, blue jeans with red blouses and shirts will suffice.

you may find a red sweat-suit

add paper hearts if you wish

All the people they meet in the park should dress in normal clothes. MS. JOHNSON and the MCCOYS should wear glasses and a bit of baby powder in their hair, maybe just at the temples. JANET could wear a dress, and Jim could wear a shirt and tie.

an older sister's dress may help age MS. MCCOY

sensible shoes

A design for wings for MS. LOVEJOY and the CUPIDS is illustrated below. You should reproduce this shape (or approximate it) on large sheets of heavy cardboard (perhaps an appliance box). Make the wings two or three feet in length depending upon the height of your actors. Cut two 2 foot lengths of rope (clothesline will work fine) per pair of wings, and form backpack-like straps by punching two holes in the wings just above and below the actors' shoulders. Push the rope through and tie a knot at the top and bottom of each piece on the backside of the wings to keep the rope from slipping through. A can of red spray paint can be used to paint both the cardboard and the pieces of rope, but allow them to dry for at least 24 hours. The actors can decorate their own wings with glitter, lace, sequins, popcorn, coins, and/or buttons.

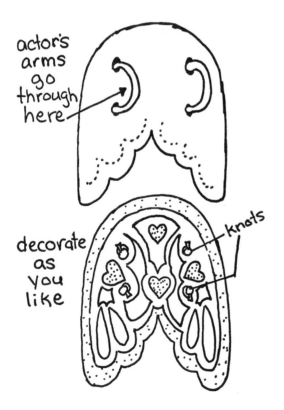

actor's arms go through here

decorate as you like

knots

TEACHING MATERIALS:

I. Writing Exercise

Several of the characters in *The School for Cupids* find happiness by compromising with one another. After explaining that compromise is the settlement of differences by mutual concessions, ask students to think of a time when a problem they had was solved by compromise. Ask them to write a brief paper describing the problem and how it was resolved.

If some have difficulty recalling such a time, create a fictitious situation for them. Suggestions: Two siblings want to watch different television shows at the same time; a daughter wants to go shopping with friends, but Mom wants her to clean up her room; etc. Ask students to write a short paper explaining how compromise could solve the problem.

II. Class Discussion

One of the problems between two of the characters in the play is a lack of communication. As a class, discuss times when class members may have miscommunicated by saying something they didn't mean. Start the discussion by giving the following example: A husband asks a wife what she wants for her birthday. She says, "Oh nothing..." The husband buys nothing for his wife for her birthday and is shocked when she is upset. How did the wife miscommunicate with her husband? Another way some students may have miscommunicated is failing to speak up when, for instance, someone hurts their feelings. Discuss ways of improving communication skills.

Words by Judy Truesdell Mecca
= 80

Music by Jenifer Truesdell Christman
and Woody Christman

"Be A Cupid"

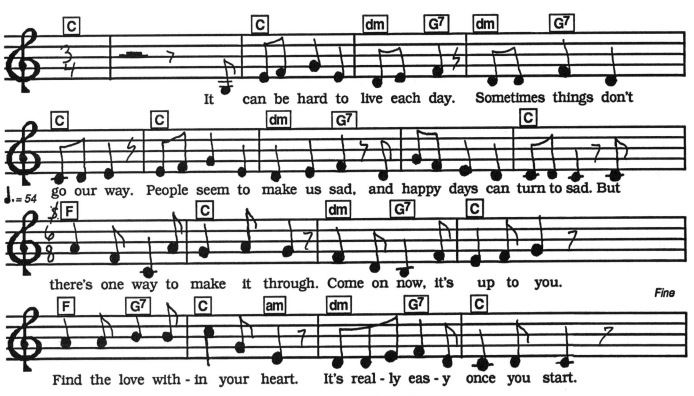

It can be hard to live each day. Sometimes things don't

go our way. People seem to make us sad, and happy days can turn to sad. But

there's one way to make it through. Come on now, it's up to you.

Fine

Find the love with - in your heart. It's real - ly eas - y once you start.

THE SCHOOL FOR CUPIDS

A Play for Valentine's Day

(The play begins in a classroom of the School for Cupids. The chalkboard reads, "School for Cupids." The teacher, **MS. LOVEJOY**, is at her desk. She is dressed in red wearing large red wings. There may be as many Cupid students as you like, but there are at least three – **HARDY, HOPE**, and **SUNNY**. They are sitting at their desks looking excited and hopeful. They are dressed in red or pink.)

MS. LOVEJOY: Good morning, class! I'm so glad to see you here today looking so cheerful and eager to spread love to the world. I'll do my best to make full-fledged Cupids out of you in time for Valentine's Day.

HOPE: (Raising her hand.) Ms. Lovejoy, what does it take to be a Cupid? I'm afraid I'm not smart enough!

MS. LOVEJOY: Don't you worry, Hope. You look smart to me.

SUNNY: (Raising her hand.) Ms. Lovejoy, I'm sure I want to be a Cupid, but I'm not sure I want to look like a baby and shoot people with arrows! Doesn't it hurt them?

MS. LOVEJOY: You won't become a baby, Sunny, and you won't shoot anyone with an arrow. We do it differently now. I think you'll like it. More questions?

HARDY: Yes, I have one. I'm a guy, and I want to be a Cupid. But I don't want to make people fall in love and kiss and stuff! Yuck!

MS. LOVEJOY: Hardy, I think you'll find there are all kinds of love, not just romantic love. You won't get sick, I promise.

HARDY: OK, but remember, you promised!

MS. LOVEJOY: I'll remember. Now, students, come with me! We're going to the park to practice with some people who need our help.

(She starts to leave then remembers she is wearing her wings.)

Oops! I'd better not let anyone see me wearing these! People get so confused.

(She removes the wings and puts them out of sight.)

Now, come with me!

(The would-be **CUPIDS** rearrange the desks to form two park benches on either side of the acting area facing the audience. They erase "School for Cupids" from the board and draw trees and the sun. **MS. JOHNSON** and her sons **JOE** and **PAUL** enter. They sit on one park bench. **MS. LOVEJOY** motions for the would-be **CUPIDS** to sit on the other bench. She stands near the **JOHNSONS**.)

MS. JOHNSON: You boys make me so tired. You fight and argue all the time, and you never do a thing to help around the house. Then you beg me for money to buy toys! Why, when I was your age...

PAUL: Oh, Mom, we don't want to hear how it was when you were our age.

JOE: We know it by heart.

JOE and **PAUL:** "I felt lucky to have even one toy to play with. I never got a new toy except at Christmas, and only then if my father had worked an extra job."

MS. JOHNSON: OK, OK, hush up.

JOE: Mom, we're **bored**. We get into fights because we don't have anything to do!

PAUL: And because Joe is a nerd.

JOE: A nerd, huh? Why, you...

MS. JOHNSON: See? That's just what I'm talking about. I'll be grayheaded before I'm ...uh...before I'm very old!

MS. LOVEJOY: (To the **CUPIDS**-to-be.) Now watch this! (To the **JOHNSONS**.) Excuse me, but I couldn't help overhearing. Children can be tiring, can't they?

MS. JOHNSON: They sure can. Got any of your own?

MS. LOVEJOY: (Looking back at the **CUPIDS**-to-be.) Yes, all these fine young people with me.

(The **CUPIDS** wave.)

MS. JOHNSON: At least they all like the same color. My boys don't like the same **anything**! They're driving me nuts!

MS. LOVEJOY: May I make a suggestion?

MS. JOHNSON: I'm all ears!

MS. LOVEJOY: You boys want money to buy toys, don't you?

JOE: We sure do!

PAUL: But Mom and Dad aren't rich...

JOE: They do the best they can, I guess...

MS. JOHNSON: Well, that's nice to hear for a change!

MS. LOVEJOY: You boys want something to do with your time, don't you?

PAUL: We sure do!

MS. LOVEJOY: Ms. Johnson, are there some jobs around your house that you dislike?

MS. JOHNSON: Well, let me see. I really hate to clean out the refrigerator. Food gets down in the bottom and it's a yucky mess!

MS. LOVEJOY: Any others?

MS. JOHNSON: My husband has been meaning to stack up all the newspapers in the garage and throw them away. But since he works so hard during the week, I have to nag him about it on weekends.

MS. LOVEJOY: Joe? Paul? Could you do some of these jobs for your mom?

JOE: Well, sure...

PAUL: I guess...

MS. LOVEJOY: Ms. Johnson, do you think you could spare a little cookie jar money to pay the boys to do these things for you?

MS. JOHNSON: Well, we're on a pretty tight budget...

JOE: Oh, Mom, it would be great!

PAUL: I have an idea! What if we went up and down our street asking the neighbors if they had jobs for us?

JOE: That's a great idea! We could make more money, and it would give us something to do!

MS. JOHNSON: Maybe if they were busy they wouldn't fight all the time.

(MS. LOVEJOY has gone behind their bench. She takes some love dust out of her purse and sprinkles it on the **JOHNSONS.)**

MS. JOHNSON: They really aren't bad boys...

JOE: We don't mean to give you a hard time, Mom.

PAUL: It's just that you're our mother and we expect you to fix whatever's wrong!

MS. JOHNSON: Well, I can't always! I'm a person, too, and I'd like some peace and quiet and some help!

JOE: We will help you, Mom. I really like this idea. We'll make a little business out of it!

PAUL: I've got it! We'll call ourselves, "Johnson's II"!

MS. JOHNSON: It sounds good, boys. I'll be your first customer. You clean out the refrigerator and carry those papers away, and I'll pay you each an extra week's allowance.

JOE and **PAUL:** Yeah! Sounds great, Mom! Thanks!

MS. JOHNSON: I really do love you guys.

JOE: We love you, Mom.

PAUL: I'm sorry we've been crummy.

MS. JOHNSON: Let's get home and get started. (To **MS. LOVEJOY.**) Say, thanks! You really helped us out!

(They exit, and **MS. LOVEJOY** returns to the **CUPIDS.**)

SUNNY: That was great!

HARDY: You really helped those people!

HOPE: What was that stuff you sprinkled?

MS. LOVEJOY: It's love dust, students, and I'm going to give some to all of you. (She hands an envelope to each.) Now, we're going to split up. Each of you find some people in trouble and help them find the love in their hearts. You may sprinkle love dust, but wait until the right moment. You'll know when that is.

HARDY: You mean we're on our own?

SUNNY: I'm scared!

MS. LOVEJOY: You'll do fine. Now run along and we'll meet back here in one hour.

(All but **SUNNY** exit.)

SUNNY: Gosh, I'm really scared. What if I don't know the answer to a problem? I didn't study this stuff in school! Oh no, here come some people.

(Enter **MR.** and **MRS. MCCOY.** They are an older couple. He has a newspaper, and she is carrying her knitting. They sit, and he begins reading the paper, and she starts to knit. They ignore each other.)

SUNNY: (Aside to audience.) Well, here goes. (To the **MCCOYS**.) Hey!

MR. MCCOY: Hello, young lady.

SUNNY: Pretty day. What are your names?

MRS. MCCOY: We're the McCoys. What's your name?

SUNNY: Sunny.

MR. MCCOY: Well, we agree that it is a lovely, sunny day. Now what is your name?

SUNNY: That is my name. "Sunny's" my name.

MR. MCCOY: Oh, I see.

SUNNY: Are you two married?

MRS. MCCOY: Heavens, yes! Can't you tell?

SUNNY: What do you mean?

MRS. MCCOY: I mean, we're not talking! We're here in the park on a beautiful day, and we're not talking! Only married people are together...and yet **not** together.

SUNNY: I don't understand.

MR. MCCOY: What the "Mrs." is trying to say, young lady, is that we've been together so long, we're...

MRS. MCCOY: We're...well...

MR. MCCOY: Tired of each other, wouldn't you say?

MRS. MCCOY: We don't seem to have very much in common.

70

MRS. MCCOY: No, we really don't.

SUNNY: Does it have to be that way? Were there things you liked to do together when you were first married?

MRS. MCCOY: Good heavens, child! Who can remember back that far?

SUNNY: I'll bet **you** can. (She gets her envelope of love dust and pretends to sneeze.)

Achoo! (Love dust blows on the couple.)

MR. and **MRS. MCCOY:** Bless you! (They laugh, realizing they've said the same thing.)

MR. MCCOY: Well, I don't know the last time we spoke at once.

MRS. MCCOY: No, but I remember a time when a sneeze made us laugh!

MR. MCCOY: A sneeze?

MRS. MCCOY: Yes. We hadn't been married long and we decided to go camping.

MR. MCCOY: I haven't thought about this in fifteen years.

MRS. MCCOY: It took us two hours to get the tent up, and then when we were inside, you sneezed, and it fell right on our heads!

(They both laugh.)

MR. MCCOY: You know, dear, I still like to camp.

MRS. MCCOY: I do, too! I just forgot.

MR. MCCOY: I guess we've forgotten a few things, haven't we?

MRS. MCCOY: Is it too late to remember?

MR. MCCOY: It's not too late to try.

MRS. MCCOY: I could go for an ice cream cone, how about you?

MR. MCCOY: Do you suppose our bicycles still work? We could ride them to the ice cream parlor!

MRS. MCCOY: Let's hit the road! Say, Sunny...

(**SUNNY** remains on stage long enough to see the couple talking and laughing, then she exits. **HARDY** enters in the meantime.)

HARDY: Yes, it is a sunny day!

MRS. MCCOY: No, there was a girl...oh, never mind. Let's go get a double dip!

(They exit.)

SCENE II

HARDY: Oh, me. I just know some drippy, love-sick couple is going to come along, kissing and hugging and making me **sick!**

(Enter **ELAINE** and **ELISE**.)

ELAINE: Leave me alone! I have got to have a minute to myself!

ELISE: But you promised to play with me if I watched TV by myself this morning!

HARDY: (Aside to audience.) Ah, some "normal" fighting sisters! Everything's going to be all right now! (To the **GIRLS**.) Excuse me, girls, do you come to this park very often?

ELAINE: Who are you?

HARDY: My name is Hardy, and I just moved into the neighborhood. This park is close to my house, so I walked down here.

ELAINE: Yeah, we come here a lot. Sometimes I come here by myself to get away from my sister! She's always tagging along!

ELISE: But I don't have anybody to play with! Elaine is my sister and she **has** to play with me!

ELAINE: Where does it say that? Is there a book of rules for sisters?

ELISE: Yes, I think so!

HARDY: Is there a baseball team around here? Do they maybe play at the park?

ELAINE: Yeah, maybe. Yes, I think they play on Saturday afternoons. Did you say you were new?

HARDY: Yes, I just moved here from...uh...from Cupidville, New Mexico.

ELAINE: What a weird name for a city!

HARDY: It's deep in the **heart** of New Mexico. Get it?

ELAINE: No.

HARDY: (Aside to audience.) This could be more difficult than I thought!

(To the **GIRLS**.) I really miss my friends back in...um...Cupidville. I don't have anyone to play with.

ELISE: Don't you have any brothers or sisters?

HARDY: No, I'm an only child.

ELAINE: I'm sorry you're lonely. I remember when we moved here. I was lonely, too.

HARDY: Were you an only child then?

ELAINE: No, I had Elise.

HARDY: So you had at least one friend to play with – your sister.

ELAINE: Well, yeah. I mean, no! She's just my sister!

HARDY: Didn't you play together?

ELISE: Yes, we did, Elaine! Don't you remember the first night in our new house? Dad gave us some empty moving boxes...

ELAINE: Oh yeah. We made little houses out of them and played "old house, new house." I guess we were both pretty scared about moving to a new city.

(**HARDY** points at "nothing" in the sky.)

HARDY: Look over there!

(When the **GIRLS** look, he blows love dust on them.)

ELISE: I wasn't afraid, Elaine. I thought, "If Elaine thinks this is OK, it must be. She's my big sister."

ELAINE: You did? But I was scared to death!

ELISE: I didn't know.

HARDY: So you look up to Elaine, right? You watch what she does?

ELISE: Of course! She's my big sister. I...

HARDY: You what?

ELISE: Don't make me say it!

ELAINE: Say what?

ELISE: I guess I love her. There. Is everybody happy?

ELAINE: Well, squirt, you know I love you, too.

HARDY: Think back, Elaine. Weren't you glad to have her along when you moved here?

ELAINE: Oh, well...I guess. Yes, it was better to have someone with me.

ELISE: Remember we slept with our light on the first night?

ELAINE: Elise, don't tell that.

HARDY: I think you love each other a lot. Elaine, your sister looks up to you and enjoys your company. I'll bet you enjoy hers, too. But Elise, Elaine needs some time alone. Elise, if you knew that Elaine would play with you in the afternoon, could you leave her alone all morning?

ELISE: Sure!

HARDY: Elaine, if you had the whole morning to yourself every day, would you play with Elise in the afternoon?

ELAINE: Yes, I think so. She's OK for a little sister.

HARDY: Good. Hey, look! (He points at "nothing" again and exits while **ELAINE** and **ELISE** are looking.)

ELAINE: Well, come on, squirt. I'll race you home.

(She looks around.)

Where did Hardy go? Oh well, I guess we'll see him around. Ready? Set? Go! (They exit.)

(SCENE III)

(**HOPE** enters with one arm around **JANET'S** shoulders and one arm around **JIM'S**.)

JANET: I'm just not lucky in love, Hope. I want a nice, kind husband.

JIM: Me either, Hope. I want to marry a sweet lady!

JANET: I want a home and children, but I'd like to work some, too!

JIM: I want to settle down and have some kids, but I want a wife who won't mind working to help out!

JANET: I really like it here. I don't want to move far away!

JIM: I love this neighborhood! It's my home!

JANET: I can't seem to find a man who wants the same things I want!

JIM: And I can't find a wife who wants the same things I want!

HOPE: (Sighing.) Both of you breathe deeply.

(**JIM** and **JANET** breathe deeply. **HOPE** sprinkles love dust.)

JIM: Janet!

JANET: Jim! You were here all along!

(They exit arm in arm.)

HOPE: Some things are just too easy!

(**HARDY, SUNNY,** any other **CUPIDS** you have included enter. **MS. LOVEJOY** enters carrying their wings.)

MS. LOVEJOY: You were great! I'm so proud of all you!

SUNNY: It was really easier than I thought it would be.

HOPE: We met some nice people.

HARDY: What's in that love dust? It's awesome!

MS. LOVEJOY: To tell the truth, nothing. It's just glitter (or whatever material you used for love dust). The real way to be a Cupid is to help people see the love they already have inside!

SUNNY: So, in a way, everyone's a Cupid!

MS. LOVEJOY: Yes, Sunny, that's right. But you all did so well. I'm proud to award you your wings.

(Ms. Lovejoy gives the students their wings, and they put them on.)

MS. LOVEJOY: You're all Cupids! I give you your wings with love!

ALL: (Musical score page 65.)

"Be A Cupid"

It can be hard to live each day,
Sometimes things don't go our way.
People seem to make us sad,
And happy days can turn to sad.

But there's one way to make it through.
Come on now, it's up to you.
Find the love within your heart.
It's really easy once you start.

POSITIVELY LUCKY

THE CAST

- **Lisa the Leprechaun**

- **Mom McShanahan**

- **Dad McShanahan**

- **Glen McShanahan**

- **Mike**

- **Ms. Taylor**

- **A chorus** *(if you wish)*

NOTES TO THE TEACHER/DIRECTOR:

Positively Lucky is a St. Patrick's Day play in which the main character Glen McShanahan thinks he is having bad luck. His parents scold him about a low test grade and two papers he did not deliver on his paper route. His best friend Mike breaks their standing Saturday outing, and his teacher tells him his attitude may eliminate him as a candidate for the "Student of the Year" award. But things begin to look up when he finds a lucky four-leaf clover. He's convinced he has been enchanted by the "luck o' the Irish," then his mother reveals that she accidentally "washed" the four-leaf clover the night before when she washed Glen's jeans. He laughingly realizes that the change in his luck is the result of a change in his own attitude. The play ends with the song "Positively Lucky."

The lesson in this play is the importance of a positive attitude and assuming responsibility. Glen has made a commitment to deliver a certain number of papers on his route and must take responsibility for that.

Words or phrases in the play which may be new to your students include:

attitude	concentrate	"hit the books"	outstanding	"spin a yarn"
blaming	consider	leprechaun	positive	valuable
"chip on your shoulder"	conversation	mentioned	ruined	

The class should become familiar with these words and phrases before beginning work on the play. Additional teaching materials are included.

PROPS

- Magazine
- Newspaper
- Pipe
- One or two school books
- Two tickets
- Laundry basket
- Pair of jeans
- Two four-leaf clovers – one in good shape and another that has been "washed." Make them out of construction paper and "crumple" the "washed" one to give the illusion it has been washed and dried.

SCENERY

LISA THE LEPRECHAUN needs a high stool on one side of the acting area.

A small platform will work as well, but something is needed to separate her from the rest of the action.

The living room scene needs only two chairs. They can be classroom chairs covered with quilts or blankets from home.

A classroom scene is necessary, but since the rest of the class is not included, use the same two chairs and remove the coverings. You might wish to move them to the far left or right side of the acting area to make it very clear they represent a new location. Leave room for GLEN to walk when he walks home.

GLEN needs one chair to study in (representing a chair or desk in his room).

COSTUMES

LISA THE LEPRECHAUN should wear solid green – a dress, leotards, sweatsuit, or shorts and top will be fine. Perhaps someone can sew her a triangular stocking cap-style hat out of green flannel or cotton. Green socks will do in lieu of elfin boots, or she can wear a pair of boots.

The rest of the cast should wear street clothes. MOM, DAD, and MS. TAYLOR should dress to suit their ages – dresses for the ladies, a shirt and tie for DAD. If you'd like to gray their hair, use baby powder sparingly at the temples.

GLEN and MIKE should wear regular school clothes – jeans and shirts.

If you use a CHORUS, it might be fun to have each member wear a green shirt or blouse the day of the performance.

TEACHING MATERIALS:

I. Writing Exercise

Glen demonstrates responsibility when he follows through with his commitment to deliver papers in his neighborhood. After discussing with your class what it means to accept responsibility, ask them to write a brief paper describing things for which they are responsible. (Ask them to include any pets, household chores, even homework.) Have each student discuss whether he feels he has upheld his responsibility and if not, why.

II. Class Discussion

Glen's luck turns around when he adopts a positive attitude. After discussing the difference between a positive and negative attitude with your class, write the following situations on the board:

1. A girl wants to go skating with a friend, but a neighbor asks her to baby-sit for $5 per hour.
2. Your family moves to a new town.
3. Your parents have a new baby.
4. The dentist tells you that you have four cavities.
5. You and your best friend are in different classes.

Discuss with the class how a person with a negative attitude might respond to each situation. Then discuss how a person with a more positive attitude might handle each. If you like, ask the students to act out these reactions.

Words by Judy Truesdell Mecca

"Positively Lucky"

Music by Jenifer Truesdell Christman
and Woody Christman

POSITIVELY LUCKY

A Play for St. Patrick's Day

(The play begins with **LISA THE LEPRECHAUN** sitting on a stool facing the audience. Behind her is the **MCSHANAHAN** living room. **MOM** and **DAD** are sitting in chairs, which can be desks covered with quilts or blankets. **MOM** is looking at a magazine and **DAD** is smoking a pipe and reading the paper.)

LISA: Hello, everyone, and a Happy St. Patty's Day to you! I'm Lisa the Leprechaun. What? You didn't know girls could be leprechauns? Well, girls can be anything they want, and don't you forget it! I'm here to "spin a yarn" for you about a good friend of mine, Glen McShanahan, and the lesson he learned about luck. Glen feels a little differently about luck than he did...well...before our story began. Those are his parents back there.

(GLEN enters.)

Oh, and here comes Glen! I'd better get out of here and let you watch!

(LISA exits.)

GLEN: Hi, Mom and Dad!

MOM: Glen, your daddy and I need to talk to you.

GLEN: What about?

DAD: About a couple of things, son. Your paper route for one. Ms. Ferguson and Ms. Stevens both called to say that they haven't received a paper in three days!

GLEN: Dad, they both have big, scary dogs! I hate to get close enough to their houses to deliver their papers!

MOM: Well, son, you need to call these ladies and ask them to tie up their dogs in the mornings! You still have to deliver their papers.

GLEN: Maybe.

DAD: And another thing, son. Ms. Taylor called me about your test grade last Friday. She said you made a "68"!

MOM: Glen, that's not like you!

GLEN: I know. I just wasn't very lucky that day.

MOM: It sounds like you didn't study!

GLEN: I did!

MOM: For how long?

GLEN: Well...how long is "_____" (insert the name of a favorite TV show here)?

DAD: You studied while watching TV? How did you concentrate?

GLEN: I guess I didn't.

MOM: I suggest that you hit the books tonight, and no television! Understand?

GLEN: Yes, Mom.

(**MOM** and **DAD** exit leaving the living room set. **GLEN** stays on stage putting his head in his hands. **LISA** returns to the stool.)

LISA: Now that wasn't a very pleasant conversation, was it? Glen felt really unlucky for even walking into his living room! He continued to feel unlucky later when his best friend Mike came over...

(**LISA** exits. **MIKE** enters.)

MIKE: Glen! How's it going?

GLEN: Not too good, Mike. I got in trouble with my parents for making a bad grade and for not delivering two papers on my route! I'm not having a very lucky day!

MIKE: Should I go?

GLEN: No, I can talk for a minute, but then I've got to study. (**GLEN** makes a face.) Hey! I can't wait until Saturday! We're still going to the go-cart track, aren't we?

MIKE: That's what I came over to talk to you about, Glen. My dad asked me to go see the _____ (insert the name of a local basketball team here or make one up) play basketball on Saturday!

GLEN: Oh, great! This is my lucky day. Mike, I was really looking forward to the go-carts!

MIKE: But Glen, my dad has these tickets!

GLEN: Since when are you such a basketball fan, anyway?

MIKE: I've always kinda liked it...

GLEN: Well, go on then and have a good time. Don't worry about me at home, bored, staring at reruns on TV...

MIKE: Gee, Glen, I wish you wouldn't be mad...I guess I'd better go. Bye.

GLEN: Bye.

(**GLEN** and **MIKE** exit in opposite directions. **LISA** returns to the stool.)

LISA: Do you think Glen was too tough on Mike? Maybe he was. But you see, he's always done things with Mike, especially on Saturday, and his feelings are hurt. Glen thought he was having a lot of bad luck. The next day, Ms. Taylor asked to see him after school!

(**LISA** exits. **GLEN** and **MS. TAYLOR** enter and rearrange the living room chairs to be classroom chairs, removing any pillows or chair coverings.)

GLEN: (Sitting down.) You asked to see me, Ms. Taylor?

MS. TAYLOR: Yes, Glen, I did.

GLEN: If it's about the test last Friday, I know I can bring that up.

MS. TAYLOR: No, Glen, it isn't the test exactly. I also think you will do better next time. It's something else. Each year, I get to choose an outstanding boy or girl to receive the "Student of the Year" award. All year I thought I would give it to you – your grades are very good; you get along well with the other boys and girls...

GLEN: Thank you, Ms. Taylor! I had no idea!

MS. TAYLOR: Not so fast, Glen. The last few weeks, I've noticed a change in your attitude. You seem unhappy, and you act as if you have a chip on your shoulder. Other students have mentioned it to me, too!

GLEN: What other students? I'll pulverize them!

MS. TAYLOR: That's just what I mean, Glen! Look how quickly you became angry. I think you need to take a good look at yourself, young man.

GLEN: (Jumping up.) Aw, who cares about some dumb old award? Student of the Year? Pooey! I don't need it!

(**GLEN** runs out of the classroom. **MS. TAYLOR** exits, and **GLEN** walks along with his hands shoved in his pockets. He talks to himself.)

GLEN: This is the worst week of my life! First my parents turn on me and gripe about my grades and the paper route. Then Mike turns out to be the basketball fan of the year, and now, suddenly my attitude is bad! Who needs this luck! (He looks down.) Hey, what's this?

(**LISA** sneaks in on her hands and knees and hands him a four-leaf clover. She looks at the audience and holds her finger to her lips and says, "Shh." Then she exits.)

GLEN: A four-leaf clover! Hey, aren't four-leaf clovers supposed to be lucky? I could use some luck right about now!

(**GLEN** puts the four-leaf clover in his pocket.)

GLEN: Now that I have this four-leaf clover, I wonder if my luck will change. Maybe I can help it. I'll go home and call the ladies with the big dogs.

(He exits, and **LISA** returns to the stool.)

LISA: Glen called Ms. Ferguson and Ms. Stevens. They were very nice and agreed to tie up their dogs each morning. Then he began to study for his next test.

(**GLEN** enters and sits at a desk with a school book.)

GLEN: Yes, I think I'm on a roll! A "good luck roll"! I wonder if they sell those at the bakery? Pretty funny, if I say so. Maybe I should be a stand-up comic. Hmm...this is a pretty interesting chapter we're studying – all about early machines like sewing machines and early farm machines. Maybe I could get an "A" on the test if I really try hard. Here goes. (He pats his jeans pocket.) Four-leaf clover, do your stuff!

(**DAD** knocks at the door.)

GLEN: Come in!

(**DAD** enters.)

DAD: Son, excuse me. I know you're studying, but I thought you might like to have these.

(He pulls two tickets out of his pocket.)

GLEN: What are they?

DAD: They're tickets to the _____ (insert the same basketball team as before) game two weeks from now. My boss gave them to me, and it looks like I'll be tied up with chores around the house. I thought you and a friend might like to go.

GLEN: Mike...yeah, Dad, thanks! These will really help me out!

(**GLEN** pats the four-leaf clover in his pocket again as **DAD** exits. **GLEN** continues to study, and **LISA** returns to the stool.)

LISA: Glen studied hard that night, and the next day he made "100" on the test. Ms. Taylor asked to see him after school.

(**LISA** exits, and **GLEN** and **MS. TAYLOR** set up two desks for the classroom.)

MS. TAYLOR: Glen! I want to congratulate you on your fine test grade.

GLEN: Thank you, Ms. Taylor. It was an interesting chapter.

MS. TAYLOR: I'm glad you liked it. Now, Glen, about the "Student of the Year" award...

GLEN: Ms. Taylor, I have a few things to say about that. I really have been in a bad mood lately, and I've been blaming everything on bad luck. But all that's changed. I'm a different boy now, and if you've picked someone else for the award, I'll understand. But if you'd still consider me, I'd be very happy.

(He pats his pocket containing the four-leaf clover.)

MS. TAYLOR: Well, Glen, how nice. Yes, I believe you have turned over a new leaf.

GLEN: More like four new leaves...

MS. TAYLOR: Whatever do you mean?

GLEN: Never mind. Thanks, Ms. Taylor! I'll see you tomorrow!

(**MS. TAYLOR** exits and strikes the desks. **GLEN** walks along, and **MIKE** enters.)

MIKE: Hi, Glen.

GLEN: Mike! How's it going?

MIKE: Fine...you're not still mad at me?

GLEN: No. In fact, I'd like you to go with me to a _____ (insert team name used previously) game in two weeks! My dad gave me tickets!

MIKE: Hey, that would be great!

GLEN: I guess I'm a bigger basketball fan than I thought.

MIKE: We'll have a great time. Thanks!

GLEN: I'll see you, Mike! Gotta get home.

(They exit in opposite directions. **LISA** reenters.)

LISA: Yes, Glen McShanahan thought he was a lucky Irish boy with a four-leaf clover in his pocket. He thought his luck changed because he found that four-leaf clover. That is, he thought that until he spoke to his mom...

(**LISA** exits, and **MOM** enters holding a laundry basket with a pair of jeans in it.)

MOM: Glen! Are you home yet?

GLEN: (Entering.) Yes, Mom! And I have great news! I made "100" on my test!

MOM: Terrific! I knew you could do it! Now, Glen, I wanted to ask you about this green thing I found in your pocket. I hope it wasn't something valuable. (She hands **GLEN** the remains of his four-leaf clover.)

GLEN: Mom! My four-leaf clover. (He pauses, thinking.) When did you say you washed these jeans?

MOM: Last night after you went to bed. What did you say it was, a four-leaf clover?

GLEN: (Laughing.) Mom, I've been a jerk! My luck turned around – I got an "A" on my test, Mike and I made up, and I might still get Ms. Taylor's award. I thought it was because of this four-leaf clover, and it was being washed in the pocket of my jeans! It wasn't even with me! Maybe I did it all myself...

MOM: Did what yourself? The wash? I should say not! I'd never live through a shock like that!

GLEN: No, Mom. I mean, I turned my luck around myself. I began to have a positive attitude and everything fell into place. What a joke on me!

(They hug while **LISA** enters and sings.)

LISA: (Singing.) The moral of this story, friends, is not too hard to see. "Positively lucky" is what we all can be.

CAST (and **CHORUS** if you wish): (Musical score page 80.)

"Positively Lucky"

The world is full of blessings,
Good friends, good family.
Don't be so busy frowning that you refuse to see.

MOM and **GLEN:**

You don't need four-leaf clovers now
Or lucky charms at all.
A sunny Irish outlook will keep you on the ball.

CAST and **CHORUS:**

We wish you the luck of the Irish
And a happy St. Patty's Day.
We feel "positively lucky" that you came to see our play!

A Different Easter

THE CAST

The Bunny Family

- **Stormi**
- **Kendall**
- **Patrick**
- **Grady**
- **Jensen**
- **Mama**

Easter Bonnet Competitors

- **"Most Beautiful Bonnet" Award Winner**

- **"Ugliest Bonnet" Award Winner**

Egg-off Competitors

- **"Best Egg" Winner**

- **Judge O'Hare**

NOTES TO THE TEACHER/DIRECTOR:

A Different Easter encourages students to show their individuality. The Bunny Family - Stormi, Kendall, Grady, Patrick, and Jensen all decorate eggs for the big "Egg-off" – an Easter egg decorating contest. Stormi, Kendall, Grady, and Patrick decorate their eggs in conventional colors, but Jensen wants to be different. Instead of using daffodils, sunshine, and rose petals like her brothers and sisters, she uses her dad's pants and newspapers to create a unique egg. Her mother scolds her and says that she should be more conventional. At the Easter festivities, however, Judge O'Hare compliments Jensen for having the courage to be different. He awards her egg the "Most Original." The cast sings a song about the merits of being yourself.

A Different Easter has simple scenic needs and room for lots of creativity. All the eggs should be predecorated. (See **Props**.) As many students may portray Egg-off competitors as you would like. The Bunny Family should look like bunnies (see **Costumes**), but the other competitors can be people. Additional students are needed for the Easter bonnet competition (bunnies or people). Encourage the boys to decorate a bonnet if they would like. (See **Costumes** for some bonnet suggestions.) Some members of the class should volunteer to decorate a bonnet for the "Ugliest Bonnet" award. Other Easter bonnet categories can be the "Best Egg" and "Most Original" ribbons. (See **Props** for suggestions.)

There is a portion of the play in which the audience votes on the "Most Beautiful" Easter bonnet. Judge O'Hare holds his hand above each competitor and picks the winner by applause. If this is not likely to work in your situation, the judge can ask for a show of hands.

Following are the words with which the students should be familiar with before starting work on the play:

bizarre	decorate	future	original	reign
competitors	dubious	normal	pale	unique

Additional teaching materials are included.

PROPS

- Containers for Easter egg dye. These need to be large enough to conceal the contents. Paint cans would be ideal, but large coffee cans might work, too. Cover the outside with construction paper, or spray-paint them. You might consider letting the students personalize their containers. Of course, there's no need to have liquid inside, just the dyed egg.
  - Orange
  - Daffodil
  - Red rubber ball
  - Eggs

KENDALL: A solid yellow egg and her decorated entry (she mentions lace and glitter, but your students should decorate their eggs as they wish). STORMI: A solid orange egg and her decorated egg (she mentions gluing little white hearts). PATRICK: A solid blue egg and his decorated entry (he mentions solid blue or stars). GRADY: A solid red egg and his decorated entry (he doesn't mention how he plans to decorate it). JENSEN: Her wild decorated egg. Glue newspapers over one half. On the other half, glue plaid fabric. It should look different. Have an additional decorated egg for each competitor.

- Egg carton
- Shoe boxes with Easter egg grass for displaying the decorated eggs at the contest
- Hand mirror
- Trash bag
- "Best Egg" ribbon (cut out of construction paper)
- "Most Original" ribbon (try using neon colors or aluminum foil)
- Long piece of paper rolled into a scroll.

SCENERY

The scene in the BUNNY house could be performed on a bare stage. Consider covering at least one desk with a cloth and putting the egg carton on it.

For the Easter festivities, you could set several desks side-by-side behind the Easter bonnet competitors and place the eggs in their boxes on these desks. Then, when the bonnet competition ends, the eggs are already in place. If there's not room, have the egg competitors set up as the bonnet competitors are leaving.

COSTUMES

The BUNNIES need ears. Two ways to make them are as follows: Cut ears out of stiff corrugated cardboard and glue them to plastic headbands. You can also bend coat hangers into ear shapes and affix them to headbands, but this will require some hot glue or epoxy to hold them in place. Then color the ears to match the

tape or glue ears to headband

BUNNIES' outfits. If fake fur bunny costumes are not available, the girl BUNNIES can wear pink sweat outfits and the boys black sweat outfits. Or, the girls can wear pink feet pajamas and the boys black sweat outfits. Spray-paint cardboard ears, or stretch fabric over them. Cover wire ears with fabric or paper, then paint. JENSEN'S ears and outfit should be different – red and white striped top and ears? Purple fake fur? Noses can be painted with eyebrow pencils and cream eyeshadow, or try making them out of an egg carton. Cut an individual egg holder out of the carton.

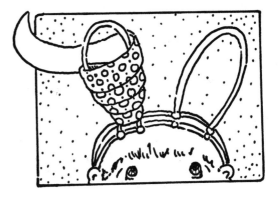

89

Affix elastic to it with staples, and have the student wear it as a mask. Attach pipe cleaner whiskers – another art project! Sew or glue cotton balls to all seats of pants for tails.

MAMA BUNNY needs a nose, whiskers, and ears, but she can wear a dress and apron – or maybe a sweat outfit, too. (If she's an old mom, her outfit could be gray.) JUDGE O'HARE should wear a dark suit – the closer to a tuxedo, the better. He needs a nose, whiskers, and ears.

The other egg competitors can be dressed in sweats with ears, or in "normal" clothes. The bonnet hopefuls should dress in their "Sunday best." Have them decorate their Easter bonnets using old laundry baskets turned upside-down and trimmed. The bonnets can also be made from lampshades, plastic bowls, and wicker baskets.

TEACHING MATERIALS:

I. Have an "Easter Art Day"! Things should be made in advance for this performance including decorated eggs, Easter bonnets, bunny ears and noses, and the containers for egg dye. Some of these should be made by the teacher and parents, but some could be made in class. Ask students to bring trimmings from home (aluminum foil, buttons, crepe paper, fabric, ribbon, Christmas tinsel, etc.), and pool resources to decorate Easter bonnets at school.

II. Class Discussion

Jensen Bunny learns that it is OK, even courageous, to be different on occasion. Have your class name some areas in their lives in which they have a tendency to strive to be the same as others (include clothing, slang expressions, hobbies, etc.). Discuss how this attitude can be dangerous when they start to make decisions regarding drug use and how a dare-to-be-different attitude might benefit them in those situations.

III. Writing Exercise

Though the competitions in *A Different Easter* are silly and lighthearted, some competitive situations such as little league sports and cheerleader tryouts can seem quite serious. Have your students write a brief paper giving their views of competition. Does competition encourage people to be their very best, or does it cause tension and expectations not worth it?

Words by Judy Truesdell Mecca
= 112

"Dare To Be Different"

Music by Jenifer Truesdell Christman
and Woody Christman

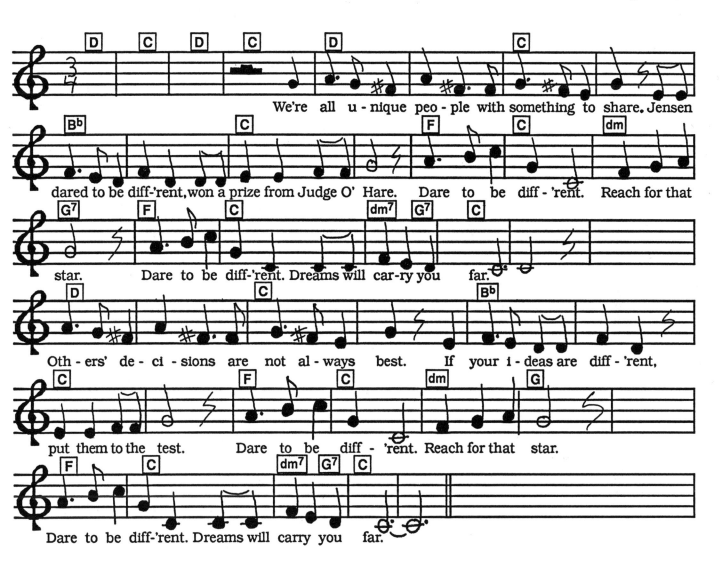

We're all u - nique peo - ple with something to share. Jensen dared to be diff'rent, won a prize from Judge O' Hare. Dare to be diff - 'rent. Reach for that star. Dare to be diff'rent. Dreams will car-ry you far.

Oth - ers' de - ci - sions are not al - ways best. If your i - deas are diff - 'rent, put them to the test. Dare to be diff - 'rent. Reach for that star. Dare to be diff'rent. Dreams will carry you far.

A DIFFERENT EASTER

A Play for Easter

(The play begins in the home of the **BUNNY FAMILY. KENDALL** and **STORMI** are stirring containers of dye for the eggs they plan to dye for the big "Egg-off" Easter egg decorating contest.)

KENDALL: Oh, Stormi, I'm so excited that Easter's almost here again!

STORMI: I'm so glad we're finally old enough to decorate our own eggs and enter them in the big Egg-off!

KENDALL: I hope one of us wins "Best Egg"!

STORMI: Me, too! (She looks in her container of dye.) Hmm...I'm not sure this dye is orange enough. I want a **really** orange dye for my egg!

KENDALL: Well, add another orange! (She tosses her sister an orange.)

STORMI: (Stirring.) That did it! Here it is, the most beautiful orange egg ever dyed! (She withdraws her orange egg and sets it in the empty egg carton.) How is your yellow coming?

KENDALL: Well, I left it outside all morning to let it soak up yellow from the sun...and then I added a lemon...but it needs something.

STORMI: (Peeking in **KENDALL'S** container.) It is pale...I know! You need a daffodil! I picked one this morning! (She brings out the daffodil and gives it to **KENDALL.**)

KENDALL: (Throwing it in her container.) Thanks, Stormi! That did the trick! Here's my beautiful yellow egg! (She takes her egg out.) May I share your egg carton?

STORMI: Please do, Kendall!

KENDALL: After it dries, I'll put lace on it and maybe some glitter.

STORMI: I think I'll glue some little white hearts on mine.

(GRADY and **PATRICK BUNNY** enter carrying containers of dye.)

GRADY: Make way for the boys!

PATRICK: The future winners of the "Best Egg" award are here!

GRADY: Step aside, girls!

PATRICK: My egg is going to be the bluest blue ever!

KENDALL: What did you use, Patrick?

PATRICK: I started with the bluest water from the sea, then I added bluebonnets from the yard. For the finishing touch, blueberries!

ALL: Yum!

PATRICK: It should be ready right about now! (He takes his egg from the dye.)

ALL: Oh!

(He places it in the egg carton with the girls' eggs.)

PATRICK: I haven't decided exactly how I want to decorate it yet...maybe with some stars...or maybe I'll just leave it solid blue.

GRADY: Forget it, Patrick. My egg is sure to win the Egg-off! I bought the reddest fireballs at the candy store. Then I got a red rubber ball from Spot's doghouse. Then I put in some red rose petals. Look! The reddest red! (**GRADY** removes his egg and a red ball.) This can go back to Spot!

STORMI: Both your eggs are really pretty, boys. Say...where's Jensen?

PATRICK: She's probably off doing something weird.

KENDALL: Don't you say that about our sister! She's just a little...different!

GRADY: I'll say! She's about the weirdest bunny I've ever known!

STORMI: That's not nice, Grady. Now don't you two hurt her feelings when she...

(**JENSEN** enters carrying her container.)

JENSEN: Hi, everybody! I'm so excited about the Easter egg contest!

KENDALL: Are you entering, Jensen?

JENSEN: You bet! I've been working really hard on my egg! See, I wanted something really different...not like the regular blue, red, orange, or yellow eggs!

(**KENDALL** puts her hands over the others' eggs a little embarrassed. **JENSEN** doesn't notice and continues excitedly.)

JENSEN: So, I used a newspaper and some of Daddy Bunny's pants. Here's my egg!

(**JENSEN** produces her egg out of the container. Half of it is covered with newsprint and the other half with plaid fabric.)

JENSEN: Ta da! What do you think?

(All the **BUNNIES** drop their jaws and stare at Jensen's egg, shocked. Nobody says a word for a few seconds.)

STORMI: It's...uh...

PATRICK: Well, Jensen, it's...

KENDALL: I don't quite know...

GRADY: That's definitely an egg, Jensen, old gal!

JENSEN: (Placing it in the carton with the others.) I knew you'd like it! (She notices the others' eggs.) Oh, I'm sorry...you guys didn't have any good ideas!

MAMA: (Entering.) Oh, there you are, my darling bunnies! I can't wait to see your eggs! They look very...(She spies **JENSEN'S** egg and screams.) Ahh! What's that? A bug?

JENSEN: Ma, it's my egg! Don't you think it's great?

MAMA: (Hesitating.) It's certainly...

GRADY: It's certainly an egg, Ma, you can say that!

MAMA: Yes...but Jensen Elizabeth Bunny, what did you use to dye it?

JENSEN: A newspaper and Daddy's pants!

STORMI: I think it's a great egg, Jensen, I really do.

KENDALL: I've never seen anything like it!

PATRICK: I did once when I stepped on a spider!

MAMA: Patrick! Jensen...I think it's wonderful that you've decorated an egg for the contest. But don't you think you could have dyed it to look more normal? Like Kendall's egg. What did you use, dear?

KENDALL: Daffodils and sunshine, Mama.

MAMA: And you, Stormi?

STORMI: Lots of oranges, Mama.

MAMA: Why, even the boys chose more normal items. (She sniffs **GRADY'S** container.) Rose petals, unless I miss my guess.

(**PATRICK** elbows **GRADY. GRADY** shoves him back.)

JENSEN: But, Mama, rose petals and daffodils are not my style! I'm different! One of a kind!

MAMA: Do I ever know that! I just don't want you to be disappointed when Judge O'Hare chooses someone else's entry for "Best Egg"!

JENSEN: He won't! You'll see. (Getting upset.) All of you will see! (She runs out crying.)

MAMA: Oh, I hate for her to be so unhappy…well…let's finish decorating your eggs. Come on, kids.

(They exit striking the eggs and containers. **JUDGE O'HARE** enters.)

JUDGE O'HARE: Welcome, everyone, and a Happy Easter to one and all! We're proud to welcome you to the seventh annual Egg-off! I'll be looking over the entries soon and deciding on this year's Best Egg! But first, it's time for the eggs-tra special Easter bonnet competition! Would all the candidates please line up here!

(All **EASTER BONNET CONTESTANTS** enter. They line up looking excited and hopeful.)

JUDGE O'HARE: What lovely bonnets! I don't think I can decide. I need some help from the audience. I'll hold my hand above each contestant. Please applaud loudly for the "Most Beautiful" Easter bonnet.

(He moves from bonnet to bonnet as the audience votes.)

JUDGE O'HARE: The "Most Beautiful" Easter bonnet prize goes to this lovely bonnet right here! (He awards the winner a hand mirror.) Here's your prize so you'll always know how lovely you are! Now it's time to vote on the "Ugliest Bonnet" of the year! (One bonnet has been decorated in a very unappealing manner. He moves to it.) I think this dubious honor goes to this bonnet. Do you agree, audience?

(Audience cheers.)

UGLIEST BONNET AWARD WINNER: Well, I never!

JUDGE O'HARE: Here's your prize! (He hands the winner a trash bag.) Do the neighborhood a favor, and put that hat where it belongs!

(**UGLIEST BONNET AWARD WINNER** stomps off in a huff.)

JUDGE O'HARE: What lovely eggs! I see wonderful use of color…and lace…and ribbon…Good heavens, what's that?

(**JENSEN** hides her eyes.)

JUDGE O'HARE: Is this an egg? Who did this?

JENSEN: (Coming forward.) I did, sir.

JUDGE O'HARE: What did you use?

KENDALL, STORMI, GRADY, and **PATRICK:** A newspaper and our father's pants.

JUDGE O'HARE: A newspaper and your father's pants. Hmm.

(**JENSEN** looks nervously at her brother and sisters.)

JUDGE O'HARE: Hmm. This...hmm. (He goes to one of the other eggs and affixes a blue ribbon to it.) I choose this egg to be the "Best Egg," Easter ____ (insert year here).
(The winning egg's owner jumps up and down happily and comes forward to make a speech.)

BEST EGG WINNER: I just want to say that as I reign as "Best Egg" winner, I look forward to meeting all the wonderful people on the highways and byways of life. I also have a few people to thank...

(He/she withdraws a long piece of rolled paper and scrolls it open. It falls to the floor.) First...

JUDGE O'HARE: Thank-you, thank-you, that'll be enough. Congratulations!

(**BEST EGG WINNER** hesitates, then shrugs, takes his/her scroll, and steps back.)

JUDGE O'HARE: I have something more to say to all of you before we go today. It is about Jensen Bunny's egg. (**JENSEN** hides her eyes again.) It is truly the most bizarre, unusual, most unique egg I've ever seen. I can't believe she entered it in the contest, but I'm delighted that she did! It took real courage to do something so different from everyone else, different even from what her own brothers and sisters did. Congratulations, Jensen! I am awarding your egg the "Most Original" Award! (He puts the "Most Original" ribbon on **JENSEN'S** egg.) Let's hear it for Jensen Bunny!

(As the audience cheers, all the **BUNNIES** gather around **JENSEN**, pat her on the back, and hug her. Then the **BONNET COMPETITORS** and all cast members sing together.)

ALL: (Musical score page 91.)

We're all unique people
With something to share.
Jensen dared to be different,
Won a prize from Judge O'Hare.

Dare to be different.
Reach for that star.
Dare to be different.
Dreams will carry you far.

Others' decisions
Are not always best.
If your ideas are different,
Put them to the test.

Dare to be different.
Reach for that star.
Dare to be different.
Dreams will carry you far.